The Demise of Cotton Picking for the Coon-Dog Jones Eleven

One funeral we were happy to attend

Vera Jones

Bloomington, IN  Milton Keynes, UK

authorHOUSE®

AuthorHouse™
1663 Liberty Drive, Suite 200
Bloomington, IN 47403
www.authorhouse.com
Phone: 1-800-839-8640

AuthorHouse™ UK Ltd.
500 Avebury Boulevard
Central Milton Keynes, MK9 2BE
www.authorhouse.co.uk
Phone: 08001974150

First published by AuthorHouse 7/2/2007

ISBN: 978-1-4259-3983-0 (sc)

Printed in the United States of America
Bloomington, Indiana

This book is printed on acid-free paper.

FOREWORD FOR MY STORY

I was born on a farm in Southwestern Oklahoma in 1936. We were a family of eleven children. There were lots of funny things that happened along the way. I started to write down some events that I thought were funny, as I have always had a weird sense of humor.

I was attending class at a Metaphysical Church. We celebrated all the Solstice's with programs, rites, and etc. I was asked to do stand up along with helping with the music. The things that I had written down, I enhanced somewhat and it was a big hit.

About the time my Mother died in 1980, I started thinking about putting all this in a book. We had some neat experiences while she was waiting for God. Then I thought the story of she and my Dad was quite unusual for their time. So I wrote about that. Then I began to think about my siblings and the different paths we took. So over a period of ten years, I wrote it all down.

After I retired in 2003, I got it all out with the intention of maybe doing a book. I was really depressed for awhile, as I had worked since I was five years old, and did not know what to do with myself. So, I got out the pages that I had written and finally put it together. I wanted people to laugh and be happy, so I tried to concentrate on humorous happenings. Of course, in the game of life, everything cannot be funny, so I had to include parts of the opposite also.

All the events that I have written about are true and none of it is enhanced as I did in my stand up routine. So this is my story.

There were eleven children born to the Lemuel Raspberry and Lottie Glenn Chase Jones Family. I am number eleven. Father's motto was, "Idle hands are the devil's workshop." The solution to idle hands was the cotton patch. Everybody else in our little community grew wheat, but not us, that was too easy.

I got my first cotton sack when I was five. It was a gunnysack with a strap sowed on it. Up to this time, I just picked next to one of my brothers or sisters and put the cotton in their sack. I thought it was neat the first day. But it turned out not to be so neat. I worked most of the day to get that little sack filled. I got pretty close to filling it up, but it just didn't weigh enough, so I found a good sized rock and put it in my sack. Brother John was the weigh master. He thought I did a fairly decent job and was praising me, that is, until he emptied the sack. He failed to see the humor in the situation. I got my first in depth lesson on honesty!

Cotton is a two-season crop. When school was out in early May, we hit the field with a sharpened hoe. The enemy on our little farm in Southwestern Oklahoma was Johnson grass. It choked the life right out of the cotton plant. My Father gave me a lesson on how to best it. You were to take the hoe deep under the root and drag it out. When I encountered a very deep, embedded one, I would say to my Father, "Now show me how to get this out again." Took him a while, but he was finally on to me and I was on my own to de-root the Johnson Grass.

One year, for some odd reason, watermelon seeds were planted with the cottonseed. Guess the object was to keep us from slipping off to the creek for a drink and maybe a quick swim. Anyway, we would burst one and wash our hands, then burst the second one to eat. I've often wondered why we didn't just carry knives and forks. Now that was a fine summer, but it was never repeated.

One afternoon, my sister and I played hooky from the cotton patch. The movie to teach us about the birds and bees called, "Bob and Sally" came to town. They even had an afternoon showing, which was very unusual. Our Mother could not speak to us about these things, but our friend Charlotte's mother could. So that was how she came to ask permission to take us to the movie. Mother was very glad to give the okay.

We learned so much from that movie and had a lot to talk about for a long time. They even showed a baby being born. We hurried home after the movie, got our overalls on and went back to the field. By this time, Daddy had a little grocery store that kept him in town and out of the field, and thank God for that! Murphy's Law caught up with us that day. One of our friends from our little country high school, Patricia, worked in town at the café. Her dad grew wheat and no cotton! She saw us go into the movie as the café was next door. Well, as luck would have it, Daddy went there to have coffee. He said to Patricia, "You ought to be out in the fields like my girls." Of course the rat told on us. At supper, we came in trying to look all tired, and boy did Daddy let us know we were not! He never did beat us, just whipped us with his mouth.

In our school, we started the first of August, and then we let out in late September and most of October for cotton picking. If we got ours all out before school took back up, we were allowed to pick for a neighbor. It was during this time, I first experienced the joys of sex, well sorta, that is! I had the same boyfriend all through high school and he just happened to be working in the same field, so of course we picked side by side. His mother was very protective of he and his brother, so we rarely had a chance to make out. We found ourselves at the end of the row and there was no one else around, so we pulled our sacks up next to each other. I guess we got a little carried away and he pulled me over on top of him. I felt this strange bump, and it scared me silly, so I jumped up and got back to my cotton sack. We picked like crazy for a little while. I don't know how much he made that day, but I made ninety cents.

Girls at Alden High School were not promiscuous and most would not have sex until they were married. However, there was one who did get pregnant and she swore they only held hands!

That year, I think it was 1951, my sister, Berniece and I were able to make about $20.00 each picking cotton. We thought we were the new rich. We got a bus ticket to Oklahoma City and our brother Charles and his wife, Rebecca, picked us up at the bus station and took us downtown where all the shopping was in those days. This was our first time in Oklahoma City and we were in awe of the tall buildings and never ending stores. You would not believe the things we were able to buy. We got matching orange dresses made out of some sort of knit. It had a pocket with a crest on it. We got a sweater, a pair of shoes, socks, underwear, and trinkets for everyone at home. Tony Bennett's " Cold, Cold Heart" was popular and we bought that record. We spent the night and caught the bus back the next day. The bus got trapped on the bridge when a big truck came on from the opposite direction. There was not room to pass. We had a stand off for awhile, but since we were closest to the end of the bridge, the truck finally backed up.

We had a few scary moments. We were two happy campers when we got home. Brother Wad met the bus on Sunday afternoon and took us to the farm. I can still feel the joy of that weekend.

Picking cotton is desirable over chopping cotton. Number one, it is cooler and number two, you can lay down on your sack when you get something in it. I have always been partial to Fall; I love the smell, the colors and the holidays. We had apples to eat once in a while when we came in to weigh and empty our sacks. They were so crisp and juicy.

One day I was over across the creek chopping cotton by myself. The wonder of it all, no one was watching, and I was actually working! After you hoe one round, that is up the row and back down, you can sit down and rest, drink some water, and sharpen your hoe. To sharpen the hoe, you used a big triangular file. On this day, at the end of my round, there was a five-gallon gas can lying on its side. It had a spout and a hole in the middle where it gets capped, but there was no cap on it. I uprighted it and sat down on it. I felt something beating from side to side, so I quickly got off, turned it upside down, and made a moat of dirt around it. My brother Peewee was working with me the next morning. We turned that can over and shook it. A dead rattlesnake fell out. That was a little too close for comfort.

Basketball was a big sport in our little country world. Even the girls got to play. We played all the little country schools around Caddo County. We had this big tournament coming up and quite honestly, my sister and I were the best two players and without us, there was no game. Unfortunately, Daddy kept us home to pick cotton. It was supposed to rain and he needed to get as much out as possible before it came. The game was to be at 4:00 PM and it didn't look like much hope for us to get to go. We kept looking at the clouds. Daddy said, "You're just praying that it will rain and I'm praying it won't." I thought to myself, "Good time to find out whose prayers are answered!" About twenty minutes later, a real dark cloud came up. It just opened up and poured its little heart out for us. Talk about praising the Lord! We made it to the ball game, but of course we did not win. The rain delayed picking cotton for a few days, so we got to return to school.

One Thanksgiving, Daddy told Berniece and I he would give us ten cents a pound to go pick the "scab cotton" that was left. We worked our buns off and just barely came in for dinner. We dreamed all day long about what we would buy with the money. We kept waiting to be paid and once or twice we actually got up the nerve to ask, but it was never given to us.

Ah, the good ole days of the cotton patch. Shortly after the Jones Kids grew to adulthood, the cotton-picking machines came into vogue. Of course, it did not do as good a job as hand picking, but it certainly is faster and more economical. I'm glad those days are over, but I still come down with a bad case of nostalgia when I motor pass a cotton patch!

THE FARM

The farm where we were raised was 160 acres in all and it was a magic place. Although there was plenty of work to do, there were lots of places to play and dream. When it rained, there were deep holes in the creek to go fishing. I took my cane pole, went down to the branch and dug some earthworms and headed out. I stopped by the grapevine tree and got me some smokes. I would have to steal some matches out of the kitchen and hope no one caught me doing it. I did not care if I caught anything or not. It was an excellent place for day dreaming and smoking.

We had some awesome fish dinners. Mother knew just how to cook them. The catfish were the best as they had less bones. The perch had a good flavor, but they were full of bones. When the creek started to dry up, we seined the fish and sometimes got a water moccasin. One time we had to kill the snake or get bitten. My brother cut it open and it had 12 babies in it.

In the winter, the snow was deep and maybe it was just because I was small that it seemed so deep. The school would have to be closed for a few days and the only work we had to do was milk the cows. We had a homemade sled or two, but mostly we just used a piece of tin or a shovel turned backwards. We each had a snowsuit and boots and would put them on and stay out most of the day. Our bladder was good in those days!

Once, the snow on the hill behind the house was kind of frozen. Wad was a little on the heavy side and his sled went right through the fence. Fortunately he was not hurt. We had to mend the fence to keep the cows in before we quit for the day.

The barn was a two-level affair. There were stalls to put the cows in for milking on one side of the lower level. There was like a small hallway to put hay in, then the cows stuck their head in to eat the hay. Then we closed the trap, so they were trapped in while we milked. The other side had four small open rooms to put the animals in to vaccinate or if we had a sick animal we put them on that side to recover. In the corners of that space were hen's nests. Once Mother stuck her hand in one which was above eye level and pulled out a bull snake. (They loved to suck our eggs!) She slung the thing and as I was standing behind, she almost hit me with it.

The 2nd level was for bales of hay for the most part. Then on the north side there were bins to hold wheat seed. We used to jump from the top of the hay into the bins of wheat. It was dusty and dirty, but no one ever had allergies, and miraculously no one was injured. When the bales of hay got low, we made a basketball court on one end. We actually had an old hoop. There was no net on it, but the score counted just the same. We spent hours in that old barn. We even played doctor with the neighbor kids in the hideouts we made with the bales.

The barn was at the bottom of the hill and the old house was further down the road. We also had a garage, a log cabin, where the milk separator and pecans were kept. In later years, there was even a windmill. We made a make shift shower below the tub we caught the water in. Showers had to be short and fast, but it beat walking to the creek. We had two henhouses and one outhouse with Sears Catalogs as the generic toilet paper. It was fine except for the shiny pages. Most of the boys used the bathroom somewhere on the creek bank and then the toilet paper of choice was the leaves or any such thing you could find laying around.

The creek was also our bathhouse in the summer. It was either that or take a sponge bath and we were died in the wool farm kids and the creek was our universe. Across the creek there were lots of trees and beyond the trees was farmland where the cotton fields abounded and in later years, a truck garden with great vegetables. We would pick them in the morning and after lunch, Daddy would head to town with his pick-up full. Rarely did he come home with any left over vegetables.

The farmland across the creek was very private. There were trees on three sides and mountains on the fourth side. I got some awesome tans driving the tractor cultivating over there. I just took my shirt and pants off and just wore my underpants. I didn't have a bra until I was in high school.

To the south of the house was pastureland. It was here that we had our baseball and football games. We always had a crowd on Sundays to come play. It was no wonder they came to our house, because every neighbor had a least one Jones kid their age. Before the pasture were the six long clotheslines. Next to the fence were some beehives and fortunately they stayed pretty much in their hives and made some terrific honey.

The cellar was just to the south of the house a few steps. It needed to be close, so we could jump in quick when those black clouds came up.

The water well was down by the creek and when the floods came, the boys would have to climb down in it and clean it out. There were all kinds of bugs and alga and once in a while a snake. I am very claustrophobic, so I could not go near when they were down there. I also had a problem when one of them had to crawl under the house for some reason.

We used to have some huge floods where the water came way up out of the banks. Our fields by the creek and the creek bank would just be covered with junk. Our house was a ways up from the creek, but on occasion, the water would get all the way up to the back porch. My sister and I learned to swim when the flood had receded, but the water was still swift. One brother started us out and three brothers went downstream to catch us. (One at a time, of course!) The swift water kept us afloat and gave us the sensation we were swimming. And surely you know about thoughts being things. We thought we could and we did!

North of the house was the alfalfa field. It came up season after season and would smell so sweet when it was cut and baled. I got to drive the tractor or the old truck while the boys lifted the bales on the trailer or truck bed to take to the barn to store for winter-feed. I was eight when I started driving. It was pretty much a necessity or an extra hand had to be hired. I preferred driving a tractor to picking or chopping cotton.

Beyond the alfalfa field was a pasture for the cows to graze in. We also dug a hole in the hill behind this pasture for our trash. Above the dump was a little grove of plum trees. The season was short, but they were mighty sweet while it lasted. Next to the dump was a low part of the pasture, which butted up to a hill. We used to look out of the kitchen window and see what we called "Dancing lights." We thought they were spooks, but I think if the oilmen would drill there, they would find a huge field of natural gas.

We worked very hard on this farm from sun up to sun down. In addition to our 160 acres, Daddy rented two nearby Indian leases. My father was a hard taskmaster, but I guess he had to be. After breakfast, he would stand out on the front porch and give us our instructions for the day. Then he would get in the pick-up and blow the horn for us to load up to go to the cotton patch. I can still hear him coming into our room in the morning and saying, "Get up you yahoos, we got to get to the field".

Dad had a store for awhile at the local little village of Alden. It was an all-purpose store with groceries, department store goods and some tools. The little icebox that held the soda pop was filled with Delaware Punch and Royal Crown Cola. There was a little pair of stuffed dolls, one was a sailor and one a soldier. Berniece and I used to head straight for them and love on them. No one ever bought them and after so long, Daddy let us have them.

When Daddy opened the store in Carnegie, he hired Wilson Gage to run the Alden Store. Once, during the war, the little store got some bubble gum. I coveted that item! I begged Wilson to let me have some. I told him my daddy said I could! He stayed there until the business closed when the small community began to move to town or shop in town. After it closed, Wilson bought "Dirty Shame", a gas station half way into town that also carried groceries. Wilson and Imogene had two sons, Dwayne and Tommy. Dwayne and I were especially close. He learned to play the guitar and was very good at it. When we had a program, he was our accompanist. Tommy was a star athlete.

In later years, Daddy also owned a grocery store in Carnegie and in Mountain View. When he finally had to close or go bankrupt, the only thing left was a cigar box full of IOU's. Most of which he never collected.

My Nephew, Boyd Smith, Eileen's son, had many happy memories as a child visiting the farm. So, in August of 2004, he bought it. We had sold the farm five years after Daddy died, as no one lived close enough to manage it. He wants to build a big barn with living quarters so when any of the family wants to visit, they will have a place to stay. Now if that is not coming full circle, pray tell me, what is!?!

LOOKING DOWN ON JONES HOMESTEAD AFTER EVERYONE HAS MOVED ON

JONES HOMESTEAD
BERNIECE AND VERA AT THE BOTTOM OF HILL

GARAGE AND WINDMILL

COMING OUT OF OUTHOUSE

BACK OF HOUSE

VERA AND FISH - HENHOUSES IN BACK

L. R. AND GRANDSON ROGER

MOTHER IN THE FRONT YARD

L. R. ON FRONT PORCH WITH ICE CREAM FREEZER

L. R. IN WHEAT FIELD

VERA HAROLD JOHN HAMBONE HARDING
IN FRONT OF THE OLD LOG CABIN

VERA MILKING OLE BESSIE

MOTHER PEEKING AROUND THE LOG CABIN

VERA, CHARLES AND 2 HOUND DOGS

LEMUEL RASPBERRY JONES

Lemuel Raspberry Jones (Yes, his middle name was really Raspberry) was born in the red hills of Arkansas. Life was hard. None of his siblings lived to adulthood, except for a brother named Jim, who died on the kitchen table of peritonitis from a burst appendix at age 26. Jim had three children, Clayton, Esther, and Jimmy. His younger brother, Custer, who was a banjo prodigy, had a high fever and died when he was 13. He was given a cold water enema and died as a result. Two sisters, Rose and Martha died before the age of five, so Martha, his mother doted on Lemuel. She and William lived with my parents on the farm until their deaths. Martha was an early Alzheimer case and Mother and my older sisters had a time keeping her clothes on her. My grandfather, William, was a sweet gentle spirit I am told. Both of them died before Berniece and I came along.

L. R., as he was called, went to Montana as a young man just trying to make a living. When he learned he was a Father, he returned home and became the Postmaster at Red Rock, Arkansas. He was a great banjo player and could play most any stringed instrument. In later years, he and a fellow fiddle player, Jim Flood, won many "Old Fiddler's" contests. After one of their wins, Jim ordered me a ukulele from the catalog. I tried to learn how to play it, but I just couldn't get the feel. It is an interesting fact that Daddy could play stringed instruments and Mother could play any keyboard instrument. Yet, none of their eleven children play anything. Guess it skipped a generation as a lot of the Grandkids play instruments.

L R's Father, William R Jones, traveled around looking at and buying property. This is how he found what became the Jones Farm. He helped Lemuel buy it and set him up in farming. When Lem and Lottie moved to Oklahoma in 1920, they had four children. Claude Vincent was six, Mae Eileen was four, Yvonne Eleanor was two and baby Charles William was seven months old. They rode the train to Muskogee, and changed trains there to get to Carnegie. They rented a Model T Ford for the journey to the farm.

My Father definitely marched to a different drummer. He didn't lift a finger to do anything in the house. If he felt like spitting and missed the can, it was up to the girls to clean it up. I think he was an original male chauvinist pig! He thought women had no place except to tend the house and never express an opinion. He did not know that woman's place is in the House and Senate! He expected dinner to be on the table at noon sharp and he would go to the table and set until it was ready if it was not served on time. He used to tell my mother how to vote and she minded him.

I can remember to first time my mother wrote a check and signed his name. We were at Kelly's grocery store. This was before Daddy had opened his grocery store. I was pretty little, but big enough to worry that she would be in big trouble. When he found out, all he said was, "Tell me the next time before you write a check to be sure I have the money in the bank." That was pretty cool and I give him credit for not ranting and raving as he was prone to do from time to time.

After Berniece moved back home, one night she was coming in from a date and saw a drunk Indian in Daddy's pickup. Of course, nothing was ever locked and usually the key was left in the vehicles. She went in and woke Daddy up and told him there was a drunk Indian in his truck. She figured he would go roust him out, but he didn't. He got a blanket and went out to the truck and covered him up.

After the folks moved to town, Daddy would still drive out to the farm in the morning in the old Ford pick-up truck. He still made a little vegetable garden and there were a few cows left that he had to count to make sure none were missing. He also wanted to check on the renter of the fields to see what he was planting and if the fields were properly cultivated.

Mother would have lunch ready at twelve o'clock as she always did. He would be back in by then. He would eat lunch, take a little nap in his chair. Later in the afternoon, he would go downtown to the barbershop and sit around with the other old cronies and solve the world's problems. He was very set in his ways and he did not change his opinions.

I was angry with my Father for years. I thought he was unfair to Mother. He was unable to show love or give his children any attention. As I grew older, I could understand that he was a victim of his upbringing. It takes generations to break old habits and ways of living. Toward the end of his life, he became more loving and gentle. After I was married, he called one night and I answered the phone. He said, "Is this my little baby?" I knew his voice, but I thought surely it must be a wrong number! I wanted his love and acceptance so much. I named our son Martin Lem after him. Pearl Richards, our neighbor upon the hill, told me I would never know how much that meant to him. She said he told everyone in town about it.

Daddy had a heart attack and was taken to the hospital. He seemed to be better, but he died the next day in May of 1970 at the age of 82.

LEMUEL

BLIND AS A BAT TO EVERYTHING BUT RIGHT

L. R. JONES

Republican Candidate for

COMMISSIONER
Third District

TREED!

JONES GROCERY IN CARNEGIE, OKLAHOMA WITH REBA JEAN,
MRS. HILL AND L. R.

LOTTIE GLENN CHASE JONES

Lottie Glenn Chase Jones was born in Wisconsin. Her father suffered from asthma and the doctor advised a warmer climate. Thus, they moved to the hills of Arkansas. They opened a spoke factory. This was a booming business in the early 1900's. The hill country had not seen girls like Lottie and her sister, Bessie. Rumor was they ran loose over the hills, and I guess it is at least partially true as number one brother, Claude, was born a year before they married. One of the church elders told my father that since Claude was a spitting image of him, it was pretty sure DNA that he was his dad. So the story goes, Lemuel got up in church and confessed his sin and he and mother were married. Guess it worked out all right, as they were married until my Dad died.

Mother had two brothers, Art and Hal and of course, the sister that she roamed the hills with, Bessie. All of them, except mother, who died at 87, lived into their ninety's and enjoyed fairly good health. Art had two sons, Jack and Raymond. Bessie did not have children. Her husband made good money with the railroad and she enjoyed the society life. It was easy to see why they shunned Mother to a certain extent. Bessie lived in a three-story house in Little Rock, Arkansas, and Mother lived in four rooms with a path! Mother also had a bunch of kids running around, and Bessie was not used to being around children.

The baby boy, Hal, was a musician and he never married. Most of the time he lived with Aunt Bess. He never had a real job that I knew of. He would play music or house sit, but other than that, no paycheck was coming in. He would come to our farm and stay for weeks at a time. He courted an old maid schoolteacher, Mae Granger, who lived south of us, but nothing except a little fooling around ever came of that.

It was learned in later years that Hal was the father of Charles Graves, who we now proudly claim as our cousin. Charles is pretty much the spitting image of Hal and he is also a musician. He was probably in his fifties before he learned who his real father was. I'm sure he must have had some suspicion, as Hal called him son most of the time. We only had five cousins and now we have six! The father that raised Charles was a good dad to Charles and if he knew the big secret, he did not let on.

Lottie had a sweet spirit and I'm sure she must be in one of the top mansions in heaven. She gave birth to eleven children and never had any modern conveniences until all the children had left home and she moved to town. She did most of the washing on the creek where there was a natural spring. Later she had a wring-type washing machine, but water had to be carried from the well. The clothes had to be hung on the clothesline, then gathered in. Of course, almost everything needed ironing. All the drinking water and water for sponge baths had to be carried from the well and she fetched most of it.

We had a back porch where we kept a bucket of water with a dipper in it. The whole family drank out of the same dipper. There was also a small pan to put water in to wash your hands. Then we would just open the back door and toss it out.

She chopped the wood for the wood stoves. One for cooking and one in the living room for heat. She could whip up a meal on the wood stove as if it were the world's greatest oven. There were no thermostats on wood stoves, but her biscuits and cakes came out perfect. Can you imagine having to fix three meals a day on a wood stove in addition to the other chores? We helped her as much as we could, but we were always in the field. About the only thing we did for house cleaning was to sweep the floor, and there was enough dirt that I sometimes wondered if it were someone coming or going! We always had one or two beds in the living room. The new babies slept here with mother. There were no cribs. There were two bedrooms, one with three beds and one with two. The old house was so decrepit. We used newspapers pasted to the wall to keep the cold out. I can still feel that cold north wind whipping through the walls. Mother would heat up a blanket and take Berniece and I to bed wrapped it in. I didn't mind when my friends from High School came over. Most lived like we did, but when I went to college, I was ashamed to take anyone home with me.

When wheat harvest came around, she had to feed about twenty men. The neighbors would all work together, so they could finish the harvest before the rains came. When one farmer's crop was harvested, they moved on to the next farm. This would mean big meals for three days with lots of dishes to wash. Those of us who were not in the field helped out, but the biggest part of the job fell on her. She was a great cook and could always muster up some kind of meal no matter when and how many showed up. My brother-in –law Harold Griffin once remarked that it was amazing how Mother could find something to put on the table for unexpected company.

Can you imagine the joy that filled her heart when she was able to move to town! She had hot and cold running water, inside toilet, washer and dryer. She did not take the old furniture from the farm. She had enough left of Harold's insurance to buy new furniture.

She took to living in town like water to a duck. She quickly made friends with Mrs. Moore across the street. Mother never learned to drive, but Mrs. Moore could. They would go shopping, and once a week to the beauty shop for a wash and curl and a foot massage. It was a whole new social life for her. The home was near the main street and the folks were even able to walk to town. O course, she needed to be home in time for her soaps. When she was older and having health problems, she would turn up her clock, so her soaps would be on. Once when she was living with Berniece, she came in to complain that she turned the clock to 12 and her soaps still would not come on.

After Daddy died in 1970, Mother sold her precious little house and moved to California where five of us lived. I'll never forget the day of the sale. She sat out in front in a car, as the neighbors came to bid on items and to bid her good-bye. I don't think she had any tears left at the end of the day. She had been a part of this community for over fifty years. She was able to live alone in an apartment for awhile, then Ron and Berniece bought a big new house where she had her own master bedroom and bath and a sitting room to watch her soaps in.

One Saturday evening the TV was on and Hee-Haw was being watched at the Mead household. Berniece walked by the TV, then turned to Ron and said, "Something is wrong with Mother, I have to go over there." So she got in the car and drove to Mother's apartment, which was only about a mile. When she knocked on the door, no one came. So she went to the manager and had him unlock the door. Mother had fallen and hit the coffee table and could not get to the phone. She had come down with Meniere's Disease, which affects the middle ear and balance. The spells would come on without warning and she would just go down. It also caused great nausea. She finally had to have an operation to cut some nerves. She lost her hearing in one ear, but at least she did not have the terrible attacks any more. It was at this point that we knew she could no longer live alone.

Her health was never very good after this and she began to have strokes. We finally had to put her in a nursing home. Here, she began to relive past lives. Once when we walked in her room, she told us to go get Chris (Violet's son and her Grandson) out of the closet. She told us he was chained up in there. We opened the door and showed her he was not there, but she continued to be concerned about him. He was in college at the time, and not very attentive to Grandma, but we convinced him to visit and they became very close. She would start smiling her toothless smile when he came in the door. He would throw his keys on the end of the bed and sit with her for an hour each day.

This concern with Chris continued. When I went to see her, she called me Dr. Amy and told me her braids were too tight and the beads were hurting her head. She asked if I could please cut them out. So I played like I had scissors and cut them out. She smiled her relief.

I was in classes at a metaphysical church, and my teacher, Yvonne, was a medium. I told her about this and she asked to go see her. When we got in Mother's room, she called Yvonne the Flower Lady. Yvonne went into trance and I experienced something most people would say was not real. They were communicating on another level that only they were privy to. After a few minutes of total silence, mother started crying and Yvonne was crying too. The story she told is awesome. She said Mother told her that in an earlier life, she and Chris were children of the Chief on a Caribbean Island. One day, she and Chris were playing on the opposite side of the island and a slave ship came and kidnapped them. On the way to the states, they were chained in the hull of the boat and weren't allowed up to use the bathroom or get up for anything. They had to sit there in their own feces. During the night, Chris was complaining, so they beat him up and tossed him overboard and she did not know what happened to him.

She told Yvonne the slave owners put beads in the women's braids. The color of the beads showed which slave owner they belonged to. When Yvonne came out of the trance and dried her eyes, she asked me to get a pair of scissors to cut the beads for good. I got in a drawer and played like I found some and she began to cut by gently pulling on the hair. Mother continued to profusely thank the Flower Lady for her help. Mother never did complain about the beads again, nor did she fear for Chris.

Later, Yvonne wanted to go back to visit Mother. I asked her if it would be all right. Mother replied very strongly, "Oh, no, I cannot let the Flower Lady come again. I am too weak."

Shortly after this, on October 2nd, 1980 with Berniece on one side and me on the other, she went to her rest as we gently sang hymns to her. It was such a wonderful experience that it took away my fear of death. I actually felt her soul go by and my hands flew up and I said, "Unto thee Father, do we commend our Mother's spirit."

MOTHER'S CHASE FAMILY PORTRAIT
AUNT BESS   UNCLE ARTHUR   LOTTIE (MOTHER)
GRANDFATHER CHARLES   UNCLE HAL   GRANDMOTHER IDA MAE
BELOW IS NEW HOME IN ARKANSAS

LIFE ON THE FARM

Our farm was eleven and a half miles south of Carnegie, Oklahoma. Farm life at its best is a struggle. Seems as if times are always hard for the small dirt farmer. It's either no rain or too much rain. On one hand it is expensive to feed and clothe eleven children. On the other hand, we saved a lot of money because we did our own work and did not have to hire help except at harvest time. Being farmers, we grew a lot of our own food. We had wonderful vegetables, milked cows for our milk and raised chickens for eggs, as well as to eat, and turkeys and pigs. Occasionally, we had beef. What I wouldn't give for those fresh vegetables today!

After their arrival in Oklahoma, every two years another child came along. James Custer, called J C or Derby, then Violet Hazel followed by John Ralph, and Harold Eugene, called Wad. Robert Dale, called Peewee, came along next. Mother was sure she was through, then Bessie Berniece (named after Aunt Bessie, Mother's sister) showed up four years later, followed by yours truly, Vera Ann, called Snake.

We went to school in a one-room schoolhouse one mile south of our farm. The older kids rode horses, but the horses were long gone when the younger five were in school. So we walked! I can't remember a whole lot before I started to school. I do remember the day we got electricity. I ran down the road to meet the kids, so I could be the first to tell them of our good fortune. We even had a yard light, so we could see to play horseshoes or throw washers after dark, or if the dogs barked in the middle of the night, we could turn it on to see what was lurking out in the yard. When we came home from a date, if we stayed in the car too long, Daddy would flip it on. That was a signal to get out of the car now and stop that necking. I can still see the strings that hung down to turn the lights on and off. They were soon encrusted with fly droppings and dirty hands, but hey, what the heck, the lights worked.

After we got electricity, we got rid of our battery radio and got one that used electricity. That was great, because we could only listen to the news and one or two programs to save the battery. On Saturday morning, Berniece & I listened to Big John and Sparky. Sparky sang in a falsetto voice and each Saturday he did a special birthday song. It is a special song and I still know the words and sing it to people on their birthday. Before he would sing, he would call out the names of the kids having birthdays. I always listened real carefully near my birthday, but alas, I never heard my name!

We still cooked and heated with wood stoves at this point. We lived on Cache Creek, so there were lots of trees to get wood from. Mother was the main one to chop up the wood and haul it in. I don't know to this day why the boys or our dad did not do most of that work, but they didn't. She also hauled the water in buckets from the well, which was down by the creek.

The boys were the preferred sex. They had the big responsibility to carry on the Jones name. The Bible clearly teaches that men rule, so why did I make such a big deal about it? Why the girls just didn't lie down and play dead is a mystery. Of course, we would have needed to get up when it was time to cook and wash dishes! And the married ones would be expected to lie down when it was time for sex. (At the men's discretion of course).

When I got big enough to see what was going on, I thought there was a mistake, I should have been a boy. I was a real tomboy. I preferred pants, however, we could only wear them in the field and on days when the temperature was near freezing. I remember looking in the mirror and bargaining with God to become a boy. I told him he could make me an ugly one if he could make me a boy. I kept waiting for the change, but it never happened. I would have been a good candidate for a sex change. Can you imagine the gossip in the community if that could have happened!

I always wanted to be a preacher, but in the Church of Christ, women had no place. They could not lead singing or prayer, wait on the Lord's Table or give the sermon. Here, as in our home, men ruled. I found my own way around this. I tucked my braids under my ball cap and went out to where the cows were in the pasture. I had a corral of stick horses and I got on my best one and rode out. I gave those cows my best hell fire and damnation sermon. I think I saved a whole herd that day. There were a lot of moo-mens!

In our family, we had to eat in shifts because there were so many of us. Yes, you guess it, male genders first. Females next, if anything was left. Even when we worked in the fields, the girls had to do the dishes, while the boys got to rest. Of course, they weren't as strong as us, so they needed it! They boys were allowed to talk at the table. The girls were not. Once I tried it, but my Father squashed it quickly, by saying, "Girls don't know what they are talking about." We couldn't laugh at the table either. My sister and I got tickled at the table once and could not stop. Our Father sent us away from the table. So, we decided to run away from home. We hid down by the creek in a cotton trailer. About an hour later, Mother comes walking by. She didn't look at us, but said, "You girls better go eat your dinner before it gets cold." I knew teachers had eyes in the back of their head, but I found out Mothers do also.

Most every Saturday afternoon we got to go to town. We were given a quarter to spend. We could eat a hamburger at the café next to the theatre, and then go to the movies. Usually it was a Western. I was wild about Roy Rogers and Berniece preferred Gene Autry. It also showed some kind of serial, which would continue from week to week. Sometimes the cliffhangers would make the week go by slow. We couldn't wait to see what happened. There was also a newsreel to bring us up to date on the war. At the end, a cartoon was shown. I would say we got our money's worth. We would walk the streets and in the Dixie Store window was a pair of kid's red cowboy boots. I wanted those boots so badly. Finally I got up enough courage to ask Daddy if I could have them. His reply was, "Girls don't wear boots." See why I wanted to be a boy, I couldn't talk at the table and now I couldn't wear boots!

My Mother and whatever children happened to be home milked a bunch of cows. Peewee, Berniece, and I had the chore to go round them up and bring them to the barn for milking. We never knew what pasture they might be grazing in, so sometimes we had to hunt for them. We used to ride them, until once all three of us were riding on one cow. She got smart and headed for a low tree limb and knocked us all off. We narrowly missed falling down a steep cliff to the water. It scared us enough that we quit for awhile. Daddy said we shouldn't ride them anyway, because it would make the milk not come down. It's a tough job milking cows. Obviously, we didn't have the dairy machines, so it was strictly by hand. There are two big dangers in cow milking. One is her tail. It is very long and bony, and when she swings it around and lops you on the head, you know you have been hit. The other danger is kicking. I have lost a whole bucket of milk when her hoof landed amid the milk and knocked it over. Mother was a gentle taskmaker and she would never take us to task over something beyond our control.

My point in telling about the cow milking is that a dairy from Chickasha came and picked the milk up daily in the morning. In the summer, we would have to sit the milk cans in a large tub. We would bring water from the well and soak gunnysacks to wraparound the cans to keep the milk from spoiling. We also had a separator that took the cream from the milk. This brought better money. The amazing thing about all this is that our Father let Mother keep the money. We bought our school clothes and supplies from this fund.

The greatest thing Mother got was a propane kitchen stove and heater for the living room. When the boys started digging the hole for the tank, that's when Dad found out, and the you know what hit the fan. He wanted to know who died. The hole was just about the size a gravedigger would make for a burial. He said it would blow the house down. I thought that would be the end of that story, but mother didn't pay him any attention. She kept right on with the plan. This was such a blessing not to have to cut wood. I remember being afraid the thing would blow up. My admiration for my angel mother went up several notches on this one!

The other moneymaking enterprise Mother and the children had was pecans. We had a lot of pecan trees on our farm. People used to come from all over to pick pecans on the halves. They kept half and Daddy kept half. Those funds went to him. One of my friends told me in later years that when his family came to pick up pecans, they hid some under the running board, so they did not have to give half.

We made pecan picking a family affair, minus Daddy. We got Sundays off most of the time and this is the day we picked pecans. First, we took a rake and cleaned off the leaves and whatever else was lurking there. Then we would put down a tarp that covered the ground under the largest limb of the tree. One of the boys would shimmy up the tree and shake it. If enough did not come off that way, we threw big sticks up to hit the branches and that made the pecans fall.

I saw my first black family one fall when I was about five. I was scared to death, as we had no experience or had never seen a black person. Our closest town did not have any black people and if they did happen to wander in, they had to be out before dark. Anyway, this family that came to pick pecans had a little baby. Mother asked if she could take it into the house to show us kids. They let her. That baby was so cute. It had white milk around its mouth and she gave us a big grin. I was never afraid of black people after that.

The pecans that we picked ourselves, we got to keep. The ones picked by others on the halves Daddy kept to sell. A week before Christmas, we took a trip to Lawton to sell our pecans and do our Christmas shopping. I can't begin to express the thrill I got at this time. To actually have your own money to buy presents with is beyond description. After the pecans were sold, Mother would give each of us some money and we would head off to shop. Berniece and I would go together and then we would all meet up at the car. It was not locked of course, so we had a place to sit and wait. I think of my children and grandchildren and feel sorry for them. They have no such treasures. We bought one gift for every member of our family who was at home at that particular time. We also got our teacher and the name we drew at school a present.

Christmas was such a magical time. We would go down in the mountains and pick out a tree. In those days, you could wander around on anyone's property and no one would arrest you. There weren't any postings of "No Trespassing". We would bring it home and put a wooden stand under it to hold it up, then decorate it. We did have some tinsel and a bulb or two, but we did the popcorn string also. I can't remember what I got, except for one time. Both Berniece and I got baby dolls and a pink stroller to put them in. We headed out for the barn as soon as we got them and pushed them around and around. This is one time we didn't have to share, because we each had one.

CACHE SCHOOL

We walked one mile south to Cache Grade School. It housed grades one to eight. It was a wonderful place for me. It had one large room, two large closets and a kitchen. There was a small cabinet that held books. This is where I grew to love reading. I read every book in that library. The playground had swings, monkey bars, teeter-totters, merry go round and a pole that had chains hanging down to swing around on. It had a well with a pump close to the road. The pump had a kind of long pipe on it with holes, so one kid pumped and four of us could drink at the same time. It also had a cellar, which we went into when the black clouds signaling a storm came up. The boys always tried to play fool around because it was so dark down there.

It had two outhouses, one for the boys and one for the girls. Ours was a two-seater, so we could sit two at a time. Every once in a while, we would find a snake in there, but they left fast when we came in! There was also a shed between the two outhouses where in earlier days, the horses could be housed. Surrounded on three sides were fields that were usually growing wheat that grew tall. It made a wonderful place for hide and seek. The school was set back a little from the highway. There were plenty of parking spaces for school visitors.

It was the center of the community. Sunday School was held there and sometimes a preacher would come along and hold a revival. We celebrated holidays and usually had a program to go along with it.

We received government surplus foods, which in my memory was mainly turnips, milk, and pinto beans. The beans I liked. The turnips I had to slip down my inkwell to hide until we were excused for recess. I was born allergic to milk and just the smell of it still makes me want to puke. One teacher decided it was all in my head and she forced me to drink it. She had to go wash up, as I spewed her real good. I never had to drink milk again. I still have an aversion to milk. I don't even like to watch someone drink it.

Our little country school did not have a kindergarten, so school started with the first grade. On the first day of school, you got a list of things you would need, books, pencils, paper, etc. Nothing was furnished in those days. The Benward Drug Store in Carnegie carried the books and supplies needed. We hoped we had enough money to get all of us set up for the year. I remember the wonderful aroma of books and paper when we walked into the drug store. I still am a sucker for books, paper, pencils, pens, staples, paper clips, etc!

I was quite a smoker in grade school. We had grapevines on some of our trees across the creek. They make good smoking if you can find one without too big a hole in the middle. Otherwise, you can really burn your tongue. My father owned a general store in the small village of Alden for a few years. He carried Bull Durham in the small drawstring bag. I used to swipe me a bag every now and then, and roll my own. Once, Violet was home visiting from California and when I went to the store, I got her a Baby Ruth. I put it in one pocket and my Bull Durham in another. I got dyslexic and pulled out the tobacco to give her instead of the candy. I ran like crazy and threw the bag of tobacco as far as I could and I never found it. I didn't smoke for a whole day!

The other source for smoking was unfiltered Camels. Kenneth Epperson's Dad bought them by the carton, so about once a week, he stole a pack and shared them with us on the way to and from school. There was a corner post in the fence that had a big hole in the middle. It was here we hid the Camels at night and picked them up the next morning. Wouldn't you know that while fixing fence, Wad and our Dad found them. It was brought up at the supper table, but I never did confess. I didn't have to, they knew whose it was. We had to find a new hiding place.

We didn't always have the surplus food, so we usually brown bagged it. With so many kids in our family, sometimes it was just a biscuit with some apple butter or maybe just butter, but we never went hungry. Kenneth Epperson usually had ham sandwiches, but then he was an only child until he was a teenager. He got as tired of ham as we did of the apple butter, so sometimes, he would trade. Kathryn Lavender always had a banana and I coveted it. Once I stayed all night with her so that I could have a banana in my lunch. I didn't really like to stay all night with anyone for two reasons. I peed the bed and I always got home sick. There came a bad storm the next morning and the Lavenders and I spent a long time in the cellar. Then to put salt on the wound, Mrs. Lavender proceeded to take my braids down and comb my hair. I told her my mother only did it once a week and the week wasn't up. She kept right on combing and boy was I tender headed. I cried and pleaded, but alas, she kept going! I looked pretty cute when she finished. Then she drove us to school shortly before noon. She made my lunch. I got my banana!

There are several other memories involving Kathryn Lavender. She and I were sparring one day when all of a sudden, she screamed like a bangee and fisted me right in the nose. Blood went everywhere. Needless to say, I didn't spar with her anymore! I mentioned earlier that we had to wear dresses to school. One day I couldn't find any underpants to put on, so I went without any. Kathryn came by and pulled up my dress, and said, "Dress up and go to town". Well, the moon had risen and it wasn't a pretty sight. My sister, Berniece, was standing there and it was one of the times she stood up for me. Kathryn got a piece of her mind, but Kathryn said it wasn't her fault, I should have worn underpants.

Once Berniece and Kathryn were in a race around the schoolhouse. One went left, the other right. The first one back to the starting place would be declared the "fastest girl" at Cache School. Unfortunately, brother Peewee didn't know about the contest and he was standing around the corner and got knocked flat. It broke his nose and covered him with blood. His nose is still a bit crooked today, but it looks good on this face.

The merry go round was a scene of several accidents. The boys were typical 'ornery boys. They liked to get the girls on and then they would sneak up and make it go fast. I fell off one time and split my tongue. Berniece fell off and broke her shoulder. She was sort of strange as a kid. She preferred to talk to those people only she could see. She never said a word to anyone, but when she got home, she went straight to bed and covered up. Mama finally figured out something was wrong. She went into the bedroom and told her if she was going to bed, she should put on her nightclothes. When she tried to get her dress over her head, she screamed. She was frisked off to the doctor in the morning.

On Halloween, we got to do art and decorate our one room with bats, witches, and etc. The teacher gave us a snack, which I will never forget. She brought juicy oranges and stuck a peppermint stick in it to suck out the juice. I thought it was the most wonderful thing in the world. I have tried to recreate it, but somehow, it is not the same.

We had box suppers in the fall, and you would let your fellow know what your box looked like, so some 'ole guy you didn't like wouldn't buy it. These were fundraisers for the school. The girls fixed fried chicken, etc, plus a piece of cake or pie, and the boys bought them. We would put on a program before the auction. Once the entire school recited "Little Orphan Annie Came to Our House to Stay." I love that poem so much, and as an adult, I found a copy. The Jones Family were all singers, so we usually were on the program.

Christmas time was very special at our little school. We put on a program, then Santa came and gave us presents and a treat bag that had an apple, orange, nuts and some candy in it. These goodies were bought with the money made at the box supper. I was afraid of Santa until I was in the third grade. We were a little retarded in learning about Santa. When he came in the door, Mother would put me under the desk. And this is how I discovered who Santa was. It was Finn Walters. His gray pants that he always wore were longer than his Santa Suit, and when I looked up, I could see his face under his mask. I never was so happy in my life.

When I was in the first grade, brother Wad was in the eighth grade. He and Joe Dean Moore often got to teach while the teacher took a nap on the bench in the back. They were usually mean. They would take the yardstick and bop you on the head if you did not give the right answer. I was pretty much spared, as I was Wad's baby sister. One day the State Inspector came by and knocked on the door. The teacher woke up enough to get to the door. She had worn overalls that day. When she opened the door, the Inspector asked to speak to the teacher. Needless to say, he was amazed that it was she! Remember, these were the days women did not wear pants.

Sometimes we were lucky enough to have an apple in our lunch and we usually did in the fall. Daddy would buy a bushel and keep it in the cellar where it was cool. Anyway, when the apple was eaten and just the core was left, we said, "Apple core, Baltimore, whose you're friend, Joe Dean Moore?" He was red headed and a little hot headed, so he always got the apple core thrown at him. He would catch it and fire it back, so only the brave would do it. Joe Dean, Wad and Peewee all had the same birthday, February 28th. I remember once it had snowed on their day, and Joe Dean had come over to our house. That was the first time I remember having a hot dog. Mother fixed them in the oven. She made a cake and we had snow ice cream to go with it.

There was no telephone at Cache School and very few in the community. All telephones were on the party line, so you could listen to anyone's conversation. The phone rang in all homes on the party line. Our number was four short rings. Another was two longs and a short and etc. If you waited a while after you had talked to someone, you could hear hang ups one by one. If the call was really important and it was hard to hear, you could ask everyone listening to hang up and you could hear the clicks! When the teacher was sick or the weather was bad, she had no place to call in sick. So, our parents would not know there was no school that day.

One fine day, the teacher was ill and did not come to school, so most of us declared we should take a holiday together. We took our lunch and headed for the mountains about a mile from the school. We climbed to a place that had caves and was known to be scattered with Indian Beads. We found lots of colorful beads, but we knew better than to keep them. Those spirits can find you anywhere you are! It was warm and cozy and we had a great time looking across the country from on high, throwing rocks and having lunch. Years later after I was grown, Peewee, Berniece and I took a walk up that mountain. I showed him the place and he informed me that it was a well-known rattlesnake den.

When Oklahoma has their rattlesnake round-ups, this is one place they go to hunt for them.

After lunch, we decided it was not time to go home yet. (No one had a watch.) There was an active gravel pit across the way from the mountain, so we decided to go there. Our neighbor, Ham Bone Harding was there and he had his mule with him, all saddled and ready to go. We asked if we could ride it and he agreed. The first round, one of us led by the reins. On the second round, we decided to ride on our own. When it was my turn, I guess the mule could sense I didn't know how to ride and he just took off. The saddle slipped and I was upside down under the mule. I held on for awhile, but finally let go. He stepped on my back. The hoof print was there for about three months. My face was a bloody mess. The gravel pit men came running and asked whose girl I was. I kept saying, "I'm my Daddy's girl." That wasn't exactly true, as I wasn't close to my Father. We were afraid of him mostly. Anyway, they cleaned me up and the truants all started home. My parents did not take me to the doctor and really didn't seem that concerned. The next day the teacher showed up. She was concerned with my face, so we had to confess up to our adventure.

Tornadoes were prevalent in southwest Oklahoma. One came roaring through in 1929 shortly after my parents moved to the farm. It took the porch off the house and completely blew away the barn. Fortunately all made it to the cellar in time and no one was injured. I'm told that when the family came up from the cellar that day, Dad saw that the female hounddog and all her pups were ok, so he said, "I guess we're not so bad off after all!" We always had a bunch of old hound dogs around the house. That is why Daddy was called "Coon Dog Jones". He used it as a campaign slogan when he ran for County Commissioner.

It was because of the tornado that we got that awesome barn. Mother thought she would get a new house, which really should have happened, but Grandpa Jones said the barn was crucial to the farm. When we sold the farm, the new owner tore down the barn and put up aluminum one.

Mother was terrified of storms after the tornado. I always say I spent half of the spring in the cellar while growing up. When a black cloud came up, she would get a stomachache and head for the outhouse, and then she would herd us all into the cellar.

Sadly some transient who was sleeping at Cache School after it was closed set the place on fire and it burned to the ground. The monkey bars, cellar, and the well are the only signs that Cache School ever existed.

ALDEN SCHOOL

The enrollment was declining at Cache School, so when I went into the fifth grade, we were transferred to Alden School. There were two classes to each room for elementary grades, and there was a high school with about 25 students in it. It was sad leaving our little community hub school where so much of our life was based around, but life did not stop, as we were afraid it would when we had to go to that "BIG SCHOOL", called Alden.

My first day at Alden wasn't too bad. I knew some of the kids from Cache. The good news was a bus picked us up in front of the house. No more walking! There was a new young single teacher, Rebecca Reddin, who was to be my teacher for the next two years. She was a very good teacher. She even gave candy treats when you did good work. Two of my brothers, J.C. and Charles were interested in her. J.C. dated her first, but I think he was too much of a Romeo for her. He was tall dark and handsome and had lots of girlfriends. So after she dumped him or he dumped her (Not sure which is correct), Charles had me ask her to do something with him. He was always kind of shy, and I was too dumb not to ask her. It escapes me now what it was. Charles was jilted a while before by the girl he thought he was going to marry. Anyway, she sent word by me that she would go. The rest is history. They married in October of my sixth grade while she was still my teacher.

After a bit, Alden didn't seem so bad. We got to play ball against other schools and when the high school boys had a baseball game, we got out of class to watch. There were a lot more programs and activities and kids to interact with. At Alden, instead of all eight grades being in one room, they divided the grades up two to a room. So there was a teacher for the first and second grades, third and fourth, fifth and sixth, and seventh and eighth. The high school had three teachers. One taught history and English. Another taught math and science and the third home economics and typing. One of the teachers doubled as coach and usually drove one of the three buses also. We were excited as even the girls got to play softball and basketball and play other schools. Basketball was played differently for the girls in those days. You played on only half of the court. Each end had three forwards and three guards and only the forwards could shoot a basket.

There was one of our girls who was not a real bright spark. She forgot she was playing guard and shot a basket for the other team. We were hollering at her as she sped down the court. She thought we were cheering her on. Once a week, we would have a game and at the end of the season there were tournaments. Our boys had a good team and even went to state once. The number of games that the girls won could most likely be counted on one hand, but we had a fine time.

We had a glee club and got to perform at the school programs as well as in churches. Frances Johnson, one of the elementary teachers, directed the glee club. On occasion, she would form a trio of my sister, Patricia Dyer, and myself. She would take us to perform in town for clubs. Peewee, Berniece, and I each sang at our respective high school graduations. All three of us sang the same song, "You'll Never Walk Alone."

47

When we got to be high school juniors and seniors, we raised money all year to take a trip at the close of the school year. We did two plays during the year, sold candy at lunchtime and ballgames, and any other fundraiser we could think of. The amazing thing was we got to pick cotton for a week. We would go to school on the bus and after unloading all the kids, the junior and seniors piled back into the bus. (After the lecture on proper behavior in the cotton patch!) We always reached our goal money wise. Both years that I got to go, we went to Rockaway Beach, Missouri. Dyke Fogelstrom would put a tarp across the top of his farm truck and some benches and away we went! If you want to know the definition of bliss, that was it! We stayed in Fisher's Cabins four to a room. Most of the kids had never been away from home and to have five glorious days with your friends brought unspeakable joy.

The highlight of the trip was taking a boat down the river to Branson, Missouri to go to the movie and church at the Presbyterians on Sunday. This was when Branson was just a small town with no entertainment industry such as it has today, but it was magic to us.

The Superintendent gave us a lecture before we went. His theme was that he did not want anyone coming home with us that did not go. In other words, don't mess around and come home pregnant.

We experienced the death of a classmate who had a brain tumor and another that drowned. The school took all of the girls to be flower girls at the funeral, and the boys were honorary pallbearers. It was really hard on us and we cried loud. I remember Red Foley had the record hit of "It is No Secret What God Can Do" and it played all the time on the radio. Everytime I hear that song, it takes me back to that time. I was angry with God. The song said God could do anything and yet he allowed my two friends to die.

The friends you have at a small close knit school like Alden are your friends for life. We go back every two years at Thanksgiving time and rekindle those old friendships for four days. Since the school was small, we have the alumni gathering every other year and we honor two classes. We also use this occasion for a Jones Reunion.

The student population began to dwindle and 1958 was the last of the senior high. The grade school continued on for a few more years. Sister Berniece went back to teach first and second grade there after Wad died. The folks needed help and she was the only single one in the family. She married Wad's best friend, Ronald Mead, that April, and we drove home for the wedding. While she was preparing for the big occasion, she asked me to watch her class one afternoon. There were only five desks for five students in a room that usually had around twenty students. I was teaching in California at the time and I had thirty-five students, so it was really weird for me. Shortly after that, the school closed and the students were transferred to the school in Carnegie.

Alden School experienced the same fate as Cache School. I don't know what started the fire, but it burned down to the ground. I began to think my sister and I had bad karma. Both our elementary and high schools burned down and no longer exist. Then, we went to college in Chickasha at the Oklahoma College for Women. It is no longer a woman's college and the name has been changed for the second time. It is now University of Arts and Science and is co-ed.

CACHE GRADE SCHOOL

ALDEN HIGH SCHOOL

CACHE STUDENT BODY AROUND THE YEAR 1930
J.C. AND CHARLES IN BACK ROW
VIOLET 3RD FROM RIGHT IN MIDDLE ROW
HAROLD AND JOHN IN FRONT ROW 4TH & 5TH FROM RIGHT

CLAUDE VINCENT JONES

Part of every saga of life is the children in the family. You already know about Lem and Lottie, the parents. So there is now a chapter for each of the eleven children, beginning with Numero Uno, Claude Vincent. Claude was born in Arkansas on December 25, 1913. He was born before my parents had the benefit of marriage. This was quite a scandal in that day and age. I am not making a judgement; I am just stating facts!

Claude was a very handsome ladies man. He left home at age 17, because Dad would not pay him for his work on the farm. Unfortunately Claude passed away before I was able to sit down with him and get his life's story, so I have to use what I remember and what my older siblings can tell me. According to Eileen, one day he left the milking cows in the barn all day and Daddy discovered it sometime during the day. When Claude got home from school, he got a terrible beating. Claude was his own man, with no hang-ups. He did what he wanted to do regardless of what anyone thought. He wasn't one to keep up with the Jonses!

The first memory I have of my oldest brother is not a good one. My sister, Berniece, and I were swimming in the creek that ran behind our house. We heard our mother screaming and this was very unusual as she was normally very placid and outbursts were unheard of. We were scared, so I ran to get the brothers who were swimming in the big swimming hole farther up the creek. Of course they had no bathing suits and neither did we and they did have friends swimming with them. I didn't care; I didn't have anything to show at that age anyway. I told them something was wrong with Mother as she was crying and screaming and they needed to get out and go see what was wrong. They jumped out and put on some clothes and headed home. I have always been a chicken, so I hid on the creek, while Berniece and the boys went to see what was wrong. After an hour, Berniece came to look for me. I put my hands over my ears, 'cause I knew it was not good news! She told me anyway. A telegram had come with news that Claude was missing in action. He was fighting in the Philippines at the time. A few weeks later, we got another telegram that said he was found and that he had been wounded in action. We learned later that he had been living in a foxhole for 365 days when a hand granade was thrown into the foxhole. He was one of a few survivors and he spent many years in and out of Veterans Hospitals. He told me the story of the soldier with him who told the Medics to work on Claude first, as he was hurt more. While the Medics were dealing with Claude's injuries, the soldier who had made the request died on the bed next to him.

Claude had migrated to California with the rest of the Okies in the 1930's. Jobs were hard to come by and he washed dishes and any other job he could get. But he was a fighter and survived until he got on with U S Borax, from which he retired. He married Florence before he was drafted into the service. After she was told he was missing in action, she found another man to move into Claude's space. He wore my brother's clothes and drove his car. When she got word that he was alive, she went over to my two sister's place. They had moved to California with Claude's help a few years later. She had on sunglasses and played the grieving almost widow. They didn't cut her any slack as she lived in the same town and they know what was going on. At some point, of course, they were divorced, but he never did get his clothes and car back.

He was in the hospital on and off for a long time. He had many surgeries to remove the shrapnel that was all over his body. He still had scrapnel working out of him until the day he died. While recuperating between surgeries, he came home for a visit. I must have been about 8 years old. Berniece and I were walking down Main Street in beautiful downtown Carnegie, Oklahoma. Claude and a friend came stumbling out of the only bar in town just as we were passing. He saw us and came right to us and got us in a three-way hug, telling the other guy that this was his little sisters. We were so mortified. We ignored him for about a week after that. He had seen so much in the war that all he wanted to do was stay drunk to forget. We didn't understand that at the time and it made it hard on all of us.

He told the story of meeting one of our neighbors, Shorty Bowlin, on the street while he was home on leave. Our pigs were always getting out and going to his place across the road and down from our farm. If you have ever tried to herd pigs, you know how hard it is to control them. Cows will follow the leader, but pigs do not! So, I guess it would be correct to say the relations between the two families were sometimes a bit strained. Anyway, Claude was just coming out of the bar and Shorty walked up to him and told him how sorry he was about his injuries in the war and wanted to thank him. Shorty handed him a dollar bill. Claude said that he could not take it and as Shorty went to put it away, Claude grabbed it. Blame it on the beer!

When he got out of the service, he settled back in Southern California. He married Hilda, who had a four-year-old daughter, Harriet. Harriet's father had been killed in the war. Claude and Hilda became the parents of Curtis, which made Claude the father of two. This marriage lasted about 12 years. Hilda had a history of a heart problem and also a bit of a mental problem. She had the kids for awhile, but the kids were basically on their own. Eventually, Claude took Curtis to live with him. Harriet was a teenager at this point. She lived part of the time with relatives in Washington, then came back and stayed with Hilda. After Hilda's death, Harriet spent more time with Claude. She is very much a part of the Jones family.

Curtis inherited Hilda's heart problem and was the recipient of a new heart a few years ago. He was working as a motivating speaker for a health food company, but was forced to retire. He involves himself in volunteer work and is doing well. Curtis has two grown sons, Matthew and Lucas.

Harriet has two children, Tiffany and Mark, and they each have two children. Harriet works as an administrative assistant at a local junior college.

Claude stayed single for a few years, then he met Virginia. She was a feisty red head, who loved to dance and party. Claude was smitten and he made her number three. They had more in common. Both were good looking and they enjoyed the same activities. Claude loved the horse races and so did Virginia. They stopped by our house on the way home from the Del Mar races. I asked Virginia how they did. She started singing the Ray Charles song that was popular then, "Born to Lose." They had a good life together. They had a poodle dog name Cozy that ruled the household. Virginia and a neighbor took their dogs to a clinic to get rabies shots. Fortunately, the neighbor was driving because on the way home, Virginia had a heart attack and died.

My brother was at loose ends after this event. This hit him harder than losing the other two wives, as death is harder than divorce, and he and Virginia were more compatible. Although, divorce is like a death! He took some time off and went to stay with our parents in Carnegie for awhile. While visiting there, he went to a dance at Chickasha Saddle Club, and there he met Veola. Veola had lost her husband in an accident when a car he was working under fell on him. She lived on a farm in Gracemont and was very lonely too. I don't think it was love at first sight, but they continued to see each other while he was in Oklahoma. When he came back to California, he missed her. So she came to visit. She never went home to stay until they retired a few years later. My husband, Gary, and I went with them to Las Vegas to get married. We had such a good time that every year on their anniversary for about 5 years running, we went back to Vegas. Some of our other family started coming with us and we had such a blast.

One year, our brother and his wife, Bob and Joyce came from Kansas City. We went to three shows that night. The first was Roger Miller and he had a running commentary with us, as he is from Erick, Oklahoma, near my birthplace of Elk City, Oklahoma. He told us he used to come to Carnegie to the skating rink. Then we went to a show at the Silver Slipper of guys in drag. It was so funny. By this time, some of the guys were feeling no pain. We went to the Robert Goulet Show and Claude and my brother-in-law Bill made a spectacle of themselves. They did not want to go to this show, but were outnumbered. They kept talking and making snide remarks so much, we made them leave. We were staying in a Hotel close to where this show was. When we got ready to leave, we couldn't find them. On the way to the Hotel, we found Claude in the bushes with Bill trying to pull him out. Needless to say, we have had many laughs over the years about this occasion.

After Claude retired, he and Veola moved back to Gracemont, Oklahoma. She had not sold her house or farm out in the country. I think he enjoyed the peace and quiet. He involved himself in Veteran's affairs. He got many an old Vet benefits to which they did not know they were entitled. They also traveled a lot while their health was still reasonable good. They went to Europe to visit son, Curtis and family, while Curt was serving in the U S Army. They went on some trips across the United States with the Eastern Star people in Anadarko. Most every year they came back to California to see their kids and siblings.

When our parents died, Claude became the patriarch of the family. Every two years, when we migrate back to Oklahoma for a family reunion, he was in charge. He always got a double room at the motel, even though he lived there. He brought in a coffeepot, peanuts, and lots of other goodies. He held court so to speak in these two rooms. It would be nice to be a fly on the wall to hear all the growing up stories that went on in that room.

Claude loved to gamble. He went to the Horse Races and loved to go Vegas, Laughlin, or Reno. The last fall before he died, he made a trip to Las Vegas. He invited Harriet, his daughter, and I to meet him there. We took an early flight from California, so we could meet him with a wheelchair and take care of him. He was a life long smoker and had a bad case of emphysema at this point to where he could only walk a few steps. On the way to the Hotel, he rode in the front seat of the Taxi. He turned around and handed each of us a hundred-dollar bill. We tried not to take it, but we should have known better. On two other occasions in my life, he slipped me one of those bills. He was always generous and would be the first one to grab for the bill. We left the next morning and that was the last time I saw him.

While in Las Vegas, I was sitting next to him at a Video Poker Machine. He would just keep playing at the same machine whether he won or lost. He suddenly stopped and turned to me and said, "Will you ask Berniece to sing Wind Beneath My Wings at my funeral?" It kind of took me back, but I know the soul knows when you are about ready to change forms. He cashed out all his points at the casino before he went home. I think he knew it was his last trip there.

I came home and called Berniece and told her about his request. I had forgotten, but when he died, she didn't forget. She deserves a lot of respect for being able to sing the whole song without breaking down.

And so, the community and family turned out to celebrate the life of one Claude Vincent Jones who made his transition to a new life on August 5, 1999. He was buried in the Anadarko Cemetery in the Veteran's Section. It was a clear warm day. After the taps were played, there was a loud clap of thunder. It was a strange phenomenon, but to the Jones Family it was not odd, we knew it was our brother with his earthly farewell.

CLAUDE AND 1ST WIFE FLORENCE

VEOLA AND CLAUDE AT HOME IN GRACEMONT, OKLAHOMA

CHARLES, VIOLET AND CLAUDE IN LITTLE
ROCK AT AUNT BESS'S HOME

MAE EILEEN JONES SMITH

Mae Eileen was born at home in Red Rock, Arkansas, on March 27, 1916. She became the first child born to Lem and Lottie Jones after they married in 1915. Claude, of course, was the number one, but they were not married at the time.

They lived in a Log Cabin with several rooms and a fireplace. They walked across the holler to go to church. They usually walked everywhere they went. The area around Red Rock was very hilly with few roads. About the only time they hitched up the horse was to go up the hill to get water at the spring. They collected the water in a big barrel that sat on the sled.

Eileen was old enough to recall when the family moved to the farm in Oklahoma. They took a truck covered with a tarp to the train station. Mother had spent several days cooking to have food on the train, as there was no place to buy food on the way. They had to change trains along the way and once when they got off, Mother's hat blew off her head and Claude chased it and got it back. At one stop, the train ran into some horses, which caused some delay. She was enthralled when the train stopped to watch an airplane flying over. Of course, it was the first airplane that most people on the train had seen.

They arrived at the depot in Carnegie, Oklahoma two days later. They hired a man who owned a Model T to drive them to the farm eleven and one half miles south of town. The Jones Grandparents, William Riley Jones, and Martha Ann Cooper Jones were already in residence at the farm.

After getting settled in, Eileen was enrolled in the first grade at Cache School. It was a mile south of the farm and there was no transportation, but it was close enough to walk. Once when it was snowing, Claude hitched 'Ole Brownie to the sled to take her to school. It turned out to be worse than walking as the sled threw snow all over her and by the time they got to school, she was soaking wet. She had to spend the morning by the old pot bellied wood stove to thaw and dry out.

Eileen finished her formal education in the eighth grade. The nearest high school was six miles away and there was no transportation, so she stayed home and worked the fields. It was also her job to cook breakfast while Mother was taking care of the babies. After breakfast, she made bread. She loved to knead it and smell the wonderful smells while baking. She did everything she could to help mother, whether it was cooking or taking care of babies.

After chores were finished in the house, she hitched up three horses to a plow and went to work in the field. She was able to sit on her plow. The plow that Daddy used had two horses, but he had to walk behind it. Together they put in and tended the wheat and cotton crops. She was afraid to harness the horses, but she knew she had to, so she conquered her fear.

One day at the end of the row, while doing a sharp turn to go back down the next row, one of the horses got his bridle caught on the limb of a tree and it spooked him and he did a run away. Eileen jumped off the plow and ran after the team. They pretty much made a mess of the field, but she finally caught them and got them calmed down. She was afraid she would be in trouble for messing up the field, but Daddy never said a word. I guess he was happy that she was not injured.

One day, Eileen rode Brownie down to the Lavenders, which was about three miles south of our house. Mrs. Lavender was going to make her a dress. While she was cutting and sewing, Eileen and the Lavender son, Lawson, were cooking dinner. They cut up a chicken and neither of them had ever done it before. The whole family got a laugh at dinnertime, because they did not recognize any of the pieces of the chicken.

Eileen did not go out on a date until she was eighteen. With our parents having a child out of wedlock, all of the girls in the Jones Family suffered from stringent rules. They were so afraid one of us was going to get pregnant. They drilled it into us so much, I think all of us were virgins on our wedding day, or at least until we met the men we married!

Her first boyfriend was Jake Fife and he had a car. He would take her and Claude to parties at neighboring homes. Once Claude organized a party for our house and Eileen was so afraid there would be a scene when everyone showed up, but I guess Daddy was cool with it, and no one was hurt!

In those early days, neighbors helped each other, especially when it was time to bring a new baby into the world. It turned out that Eileen had nursing skills and the neighbors took notice and began to hire her when new babies came or people became shut-ins for whatever reason. She was paid $2.00 a week for her services. She had several jobs with different neighbors. (Early Home Health Care!)

Dr. Cantrell was the local doctor in Carnegie. He would be called only under dire conditions. When he was called to the home where Eileen was working, he would teach her how to have proper hygiene and how to dress wounds and etc. He quickly saw her abilities and when he decided to move to a town about seventy five miles away, he offered to take her with him. He told her she could go to high school in the day and do her work in the evening. It would have been a great opportunity, but Daddy would not let her go. He said it was too far and he needed her on the farm.

Eileen got into some interesting situations while working for different families. One wife who was bedfast would only get up when Eileen would read the Bible to them. The husband would yell out to her, "Get up and come into the kitchen, Eileen is ready to read the Bible." At another home where the wife was bedfast, the husband kept trying to get Eileen to go out to the barn with him. His excuse was he wanted to weigh her. She never did go and when she was telling me the story, she said, "Can you believe that old fart?"

At one home, the wife had had three caesarians. All three were boys. Only one of them lived. On the last one, the incision would not heal, so they came and got Eileen. She had to dress the incision three times a day. By the time, they came to get her, the baby was crawling around. Every time he needed to potty, he would slip out of his diaper and go on the floor. There was little food in this household for Eileen to cook. Usually it was just a one-dish meal, like pinto beans or fried potatoes.

Times were very hard during this depression time. Daddy put the car up on blocks because they had no money for gas. A neighbor came by once a week in a wagon with two horses to take Daddy to town. He would load up a milk can full of cream to sell. He would buy what groceries he could afford. We were luckier than most as we had chickens and eggs. We made a vegetable garden in the summer and Mother would can and put the jars in the cellar for winter. We also had potatoes and apples down there. Poke Salad grew wild on our creek. It is kind of like spinach and mostly only Mother and Dad would eat it! Mother could make wonderful bread with a little flour and the grease from bacon. She would make corn bread from scratch. A pot of pinto beans and cornbread was a feast most of the Jones Kids enjoy even today. Sometimes we even had a chocolate cake with the beans. Peewee discovered the cake tasted great with pinto beans poured over it!

The Smith kids that lived over on the next section were going to Canadian, Texas to pick cotton for their brother Jim. Since it was only for a few weeks, Eileen and Yvonne were able to go. They slept on the floor in Jim's house. The cotton was what we call scab cotton as it mostly the leftovers from the first picking. They made very little money, but some was better than none.

We had a lot of wild turkeys on the farm, so the spring after the cotton-picking trip, Eileen made them her project. She watched where they laid their eggs, then put a chicken egg in their nest to replace the turkey eggs. The hens that sat on them did not know they were hatching turkeys or there might have been a rebellion! In a few months, she had a lot of turkeys. They loaded them up and took them to Hobart and sold them. Eileen bought a three-piece suit for herself and a coat for Yvonne with her earnings. She had a little spending money left over.

Later that fall, Eileen was invited to a quilting bee at Mrs. Sharp's, who lived north of Carnegie. She had a daughter who was ill in Graham, Texas. Mrs. Sharp was keeping this daughter's five-year-old son, as his mother was unable to care for him. Mrs. Sharp talked Eileen into going to Graham to nurse Mrs. Maynard, the daughter. The son was sent back to Graham when Eileen left to take care of them. She was paid $5.00 a week. The husband of the household was manager of the cotton gin there. He had a terrible temper and he would go rant and rave in the invalid's room, then came out and told Eileen to go in there and calm her down.

West Texas is a wind blowing dusty community. Eileen states the house was covered in dust on the floors and furniture. When the

Maynards went to Lubbock to go to the Doctor, Eileen scrubbed and polished the floors and cleaned all the furniture. The Maynards were very pleased when they returned home. Eileen did not know the nature of her illness until after she left there. It was tuberculosis of the blood. It's a good thing that Eileen was trained in good hygiene and always washed her hands after nursing her. The son, Don Maynard, turned out to be a very famous pro football player.

There were two churches in Graham, Texas, and one of them was a Church of Christ. It was here that Eileen was baptized. After church, on occasion, she would be invited home with some of the girls for Sunday dinner. She said every home she went to had a Negro maid.

Once a week, she had to drive to Port, Texas, to do the laundry. It was decided that she should have a driver's license. When she went to take the test she got stuck in a sand dune. She thought that would cause her not to pass the test, but the examiner said everyone in Texas gets stuck in sand or mud sooner or later.

Eileen stayed in Graham for about a year. When she came home at Easter, her boyfriend, Albert McBride, proposed to her, but she said no and went back to Texas and stayed until winter. Brother Claude had asked her to come to California and told her she could make $5.00 a week. Lois Mead and her husband and brother were going to California and they invited Eileen to ride along. Once they arrived, they took her down to the Social Security Office and she got her card to work. While she was staying with Lois, her husband and his friends went out to a gambling boat that was located a distance from the shore. Eileen was amazed when one of the guys came home and showed her a whole hat full of money.

At Christmas time Claude was living in the Irwin Hotel in Torrance. He invited Eileen to come stay there for a couple of weeks while his roommate went back to Ohio for the holidays. While she was living there, she followed the maid around and learned how to do her job, but there was no openings at the time.

Her first job in California was with a couple in Rolling Hills. She kept the house and served the meals. When they were ready for the second course, they would ring a bell. They had a little boy that hopped around like a monkey. He would get in front of Eileen and make noises like a monkey. The family had wanted to hire a couple when they hired Eileen, but none were available. They wanted a maid and a grounds-man. When they found one, Eileen was free to go to the next job.

The next job was in Hermosa Beach very near the beach. The couple had two children and she was maid, as well as nanny. She slept in a step down room where the furnace was. In addition to the furnace noise, she could hear the waves from the ocean breaking on the shore. Times were really hard and she remembers hobos coming to the door begging for food. The lady of the house always gave them something to eat. The wife planned the meals, but Eileen cooked them and cleaned up afterwards. She also did the family laundry. She would snuggle with the children in the evening and read them stories before they went to sleep.

During the time, she was working in Hermosa Beach, Mrs. Winters from the Irwin Hotel called and said the maid job was open and wondered if Eileen would like it. She did! She checked out the laundry, made the beds, and cleaned the rooms. She did Mrs. Winter's hair and nails every Friday, then Mrs. Winter's would take her to dinner. Mrs. Winters treated Eileen like she was family. Her sister-in-law was installed as Worthy Matron at Eastern Star and Eileen was taken to the festivities. This made her recall that Grandma Jones had a pin from the Eastern Star, as she was a participant. She remembers seeing the pin in the big trunk where all the "good stuff" was kept, but does not know what happened to it.

While living at the hotel, Eileen did services for the men who lived there. No, not that kind of service, but taking care of their laundry and etc. And for these services they would give her a tip. One man, a photographer, had her help develop his pictures and paid her for doing this. Mrs. Winter's brother was a resident there. He had his own orchestra and they had a gig in Germany. His ship caught on fire while traveling there and it made him lose his mind. Eileen shaved him daily and cut his hair when needed. She did his laundry and would climb up on the roof to hang it out. This was extra pay.

Eileen worked very happily here for two years. Then some old family friends that lived in Escondido wanted her to come down and pick oranges for fifty cents an hour. By this time, Yvonne had come to California, so they decided to go down there and make the big money. Orange picking had two seasons, one for Valencias and one for Navals. Between the seasons, they would catch a ride with someone or ride the Greyhound back to Oklahoma and draw unemployment. They didn't find any jobs for Yvonne, but they kept trying to send Eileen to Oklahoma City to take care of sick people. We lived so far out in the country and there was no transportation, so she avoided working while there.

After the second season of orange picking, the sisters went back to Torrance. Here they aided in the war effort by working at a diamond plant. Yvonne crushed the diamonds with a hammer and Eileen made round blades from the diamonds to cut steel. Violet also worked there later. They made fifty cents an hour.

They started going to the Church of Christ in Torrance. It was here that they met Harold Griffin. He was living with the Smith Family in Redondo Beach. He had grown up with the Smith son, Glen, in Missouri before they all moved to California. Harold went home after meeting the beautiful Jones Sisters and told Glen how pretty they were with gorgeous complexions. This led to a double date. Harold told Glen that since he met them first, he got to pick, and he picked Eileen. When the guys came to pick the girls up, Glen got in the back seat. Yvonne stepped aside and indicated Eileen was to get in the back. In order to avoid a scene, Eileen got in the back. Eileen said Yvonne always tried to take her boyfriends away and I guess this pretty much proves it!

The foursome started going skating every Saturday night. Glen and Harold were pros, skating backwards and generally showing off. Eileen was still getting railroaded in the back seat with Glen. One night after skating, she asked him if he was coming to church in the morning. He replied, "No one is going to tell me I have to go to church. My mother and aunt told me not to get involved in the Church of Christ." Eileen replied, "Let me tell you something Glen, your mother and aunt are not going to stand before the judgement seat of God to answer for you. Your life in the hereafter depends on what you do, not them." He was in church the next morning! From then on, they went to church together three times a week.

Yvonne married Harold Griffin on July 4th, 1943 and Eileen married Glen Smith on May 28th, 1944.

Glen worked at Armco Steel in Torrance, California for 35 years. When they first married, they rented a place where they could have a garden and raised all kinds of good vegetables and rabbits. They had one son, Boyd Lynn. He had a dog-named Sporty. This dog was a close companion to Boogie. Don't know how Boyd got the nickname, but that is what he was called growing up. There are some great pictures with he and Sporty drinking out of the same water tap. Boyd is married to Linda and they have three children, Jon, Jamie and Tisha and four grandchildren. Boyd and Linda are retired and taking good care of their elderly parents. They soon saved up enough money to buy a home with a big back yard where they could continue to have a garden. Glen has a green thumb and beautiful flowers were everywhere in the front yard and back. He still has those flowers growing around the house.

They lived in this home until 1966 when they purchased a new home with all the appliances built in. There were two bathrooms, so there was no waiting in line! Boyd was drafted into the Army soon after they moved here and was sent to Vietnam, where he was wounded. Those were anxious times for the Smith Family, but in the end, everything was fine as fine could be with the soldiers who served in Vietnam.

Eileen did not work outside the home. She had dinner ready when Glen got home and packed his lunch and took very good care of he and Boyd. After Glen retired, he kept on making a garden every year. His tomatoes were awesome and plentiful. They celebrated their 50th wedding anniversary in 1994. Boyd gave them a wonderful party at the Cheesecake Factory. We put together a great program with a life video and entertainment. The food buffet was great and it was a nice celebration.

Glen had a stroke a few years ago and it has slowed him down somewhat, but he is still able to get around. He was property manager for the next door neighbor as well as tending a big garden. Boyd has assumed the property management, but alas, the garden is no more.

EILEEN AND DADDY

GLEN AND EILEEN ANNOUNCE ENGAGEMENT

GLEN AND EILEEN IN JONES ALFALFA FIELD

YVONNE ELEANOR JONES GRIFFIN

Yvonne was number three in the pecking order. She was born December 23, 1917. She was very beautiful and had lots of boyfriends and according to Eileen, a lot of them were Eileen's first! I don't remember a lot about her while I was growing up, but I'm told as a baby, she was my main caretaker. I was a sickly baby because I was allergic to milk products. I'm told she would take me down to the creek, put me in the cool water, and then walk me among the trees until I fell asleep.

The oldest three of the Jones children were not able to attend high school. But like Eileen and Claude before her, she did finish the eighth grade. Once she got married, she never worked outside the home. Of course, birthing and taking care of six children is no small feat. And being the minister's wife is no cakewalk either! You have to keep up a certain appearance and a pox on you if your children misbehave.

I was very young when she left home. She went to California with Eileen and they worked in factories and did house cleaning. It was here that she met Harold Griffin who was studying to be a Church of Christ minister. Their story of meeting is written about in Eileen's part of the Jones History. They married on July 4, 1943.

Sandra Ann Griffin was born December 19, 1944. She was the first grandchild in the Jones Family. I submitted the name Sandra Sue for her. They took the Sandra, but used Ann, which was even better, as that is my middle name. Sandy was such a great kid, and when they brought her to the farm for her first visit, she was royally spoiled. I got ticked when someone other than myself held her and paid attention. After all, I practically named her and didn't that give me some rights!

Harold was taking classes at Pepperdine while working at Armco Steel. Later, he transferred to Harding College in Searcy, Arkansas. He didn't want to go to Pepperdine because they had a basketball team, and in his belief system, church schools should not have sports. He went to Harding until he qualified to be a minister of the Church of Christ. He was part of the church that was more conservative. After this, he began ministering at many different churches. Over the years, they had five more children. Her sons, Ronald David and Joe Harold are both Church of Christ ministers. Sandy worked with seniors in Lone Wolf and then at the bank in Hobart. She recently retired. Letitia Carol is the Kiowa County Tax Assessor. Venita is an RN and Melissa is a housewife and part owner in a restaurant.

Harold was a fisherman, which fit in well with his occupation, because he had lots of spare time. He was also a camera buff and loved to take pictures. Particularly sexy ones of Yvonne in black negligee posed like a movie star.

When they were in Dekalb, Texas, Yvonne made a phone call home. She told Mother, "You once said if I ever needed you, you would come. Well, I need you now, please come." Mother asked her what seemed to be the problem. She said, " I can't tell you, just come." I was a junior in high school and my parents took me out of school to drive them. When we arrived there the next afternoon, Harold was surprised to see us, as he did not know she had called. He went to the store and when he left Daddy asked Yvonne what seemed to be the problem. She told him that she thought Harold was losing his mind.

We had supper and went to bed. The next morning, Mother was in the back yard, and I went out and I could see she had been crying. I asked her what was wrong. She said, "Can't you tell Yvonne is having a mental breakdown." We stayed one more day, then we brought her and the two girls, Sandy and Letitia, home with us. She only had the two children at the time.

When we got home, I was getting dressed to go sing with the Alden High School Glee Club at the Baptist Church Revival. She came into my bedroom and said to me, "Vera, be careful and don't mess up your life like I have." I didn't know quite what to say. I had not experienced anyone with a mental illness disease, and that is exactly what it is, a disease. It is controllable by medication, but first you have to be diagnosed and then you have to religiously take the medication.

My parents took her to Elk City Hospital for a thorough physical, hoping it was something physical causing the problem, but unfortunately, physically she was fine. Soon after, she was in the hospital in Oklahoma City for shock treatments and she was in and out of mental hospitals several times after that. She would be fine for awhile but she had four more children while she was dealing with this illness. We thought Harold should have been more careful, since he knew what her condition was.

Those two little girls were so cute. I was watching them while the folks took Yvonne to Elk City. We were playing in the water down on the creek. The next thing I knew, Letitia (called Tish) was baptizing Sandy. She dunked her under before I could get there. She had a lisp and she said, "Dandy, I babtize you in de name of Jedus Chris for the remission of your sins." You can tell they are preacher's daughters!

When Melissa was just a baby, Yvonne had another breakdown and just left the house and walked off. They were in Lone Wolf, Oklahoma at the time. She could not be found. I just happened to be in Carnegie on a visit at the time. Harold called us and wanted to know if she had showed up there, and that's how we found out about it. His friend worked at a radio station in Hobart and periodically during the day they made an announcement and would ask for help in finding her. It was a strange sensation to hear that on the radio about my own sister. I felt so helpless. Mother cried all day. A farmer found her when he was out plowing. She was in a pasture sitting under a tree. The authorities were called and of all things, they took her to jail. Mother actually wailed at this. She kept saying, she is not a criminal, she is just ill. They explained that it was a law and she was a danger to herself. She would have to agree to be committed and she agreed the next day and was taken to a facility in Woodward, Oklahoma. She did get better there and was good to take her medication most of the time.

They lived in many different places during Harold's ministry. Most of the time they were in Kansas, Oklahoma, and Texas and once in Tennessee. As the girls got older, a lot of the household chores fell to them. I can remember one time when they were in Tuttle, Oklahoma and Yvonne was away for treatment again. Harold came to OCW where Berniece and I were in school and picked us up to go Oklahoma City to the circus. Sandy must have been about twelve. She had on an apron and was cooking lunch. She looked at us and said, "I can't get much done because this little one wants to be carried all the time". She had the baby on her hip as she said this.

These six Griffin kids are about the sweetest and neatest kids you will ever meet. I think because of all the problems with Yvonne and the constant moving, they formed an unbreakable bond with each other. They are still active in the Church Of Christ. They are very close and get together often, although they live in different states. Sandy and Tish are in Oklahoma, so we do get to see them when we go back home.

Yvonne developed lymphoma cancer. She spent time in the hospital and had chemotherapy treatments, which made her very ill. She got a bad cold and that set her back. She called Violet and asked her to come and stay with her for awhile. They were living in Ft. Scott, Kansas at the time. Violet flew into Kansas City, and Joyce and Bob drove her down to Ft Scott. They were distressed when they saw her as they recognized she was near the end. They told Harold she needed to be in the hospital. He finally agreed and called the Doctor and set it up. Harold and Violet drove her to KU Medical Center and Joe met them there. Violet said Yvonne kept asking if Joe was there. She was so happy to see him. All the children got to come and see her while she was on the last stages of her life. She put up a good fight, but succumbed June 4, 1985. Harold died on November 4, 2004.

SINGLE GIRLS IN CALIFORNIA, YVONNE AND EILEEN

YVONNE POSING FOR PHOTOGRAPHER HAROLD

YVONNE AND HAROLD

GRIFFIN FAMILY - TISH,
SANDY, RON, JOE, YVONNE
AND HAROLD.
VENITA AND MELISSA CAME
LATER

CHARLES WILLIAM JONES

Charles, nicknamed Skeeter, was the quiet introspective type. He went around humming to himself. He was protective of Violet to keep J.C. from wrecking her dollhouses, and he would spend time with her and engage in their make believe games. I didn't get the chance to talk to Charles about his childhood and the experiences he had before he died in 2004.

When Charles was a teenager, he and JC came down with Typhoid Fever. JC recovered fairly quickly, but Charles did not. He saw a tomato and wanted to eat it. He begged Violet to get it for him and she did. He had a set back and almost died. I think it had something to do with the acid in the tomato or the thick skin on it. He had bad leg cramps and Violet would rub them for hours. Charles was prone to illness growing up, but he finally enjoyed fairly good health.

Charles had a beautiful tenor voice and he was the tenor for the Jones Boys Quartet. Our Father used to teach singing schools using the note shapes. By the time the younger kids came along, he had stopped this, but the older kids were forced to learn. They boys would sing at school functions or anywhere they were asked. There used to be hymn singing conventions, where groups performed as well as group singing. I can remember going to a lot of them, but I was more interested in seeing my boyfriend than I was in the singing. They don't do those kinds of things anymore. However, every two years, when Alden School has its reunion, we have a sing on Friday night and then the banquet on Saturday night.

Charles taught me the first song I ever learned, "You are my Sunshine". I thought he made it up, because he was always making up songs, but later I heard it on the radio. He and John always went around playing a make believe piano and singing or humming.

One day while he and I were sitting in the house, a bunch of Indians came walking through our yard. Like I said before, there were "No Trespassing" signs anywhere and people just took any short cut they could. Anyway, Charles started singing, "Onke Ponka Puda Day" real loud. I was so scared. I thought they might come in and scalp us, but they looked straight ahead and ignored us.

Charles was drafted in the army during World War II. He was assigned to Dirigibles (airships) at a base in Vallejo, California. He also spent time in Germany. When he was discharged from the service, my dad opened a grocery store in Mountain View and he and J.C. managed it.

It was during this time, he met Rebecca, who was my teacher at Alden School. Before he started dating her, he was dating a girl, who was in his class in high school. He had bought a diamond ring for her and he went to Oklahoma City where she was living to give it to her. When he got there, she dashed his hopes and told him she was in love with someone else. She didn't know he had a ring in his pocket. He was home two hours later and the dejection on his face told us all we needed to know.

When he started dating Rebecca, the smile returned to his face. He asked her to marry him. (With a new different diamond, of course!) They were married in the Church of Christ in Mountain View on October 18, 1947. They rented the Barney place across the creek and over the field from our farm. Rebecca rode the bus to school and Charles drove to work in Mountain View.

The following year they moved to Weatherford, Oklahoma and Charles used his GI Bill to go to Southwestern State. He got his Bachelors degree in elementary education. They moved to Oklahoma City, where both taught in the public schools until they retired.

They welcomed their first child, Charles William II, on August 3, 1953. Charla Ann came along March 5, 1957. Little Charles, as we call him, is an entrepreneur with his fingers in lots of pies and is very successful. He produces entertainment programs for Oklahoma City and for awhile had his own TV Show there. He also schedules acts for Disneyworld in Orlando. Charla is a registered nurse in Oklahoma City.

They didn't come to visit at the farm very much. Rebecca was terrified of spiders and there were plenty in the old farmhouse. It seemed odd to the rest of us, particularly the ones of us who lived in California, that they couldn't come down and spend some time with us. They lived two hours away and we lived two days away. They would arrive just before the program started at the Alden/Jones reunion that occurred every two years, and leave shortly after it was over.

Charles was a deacon in the Mayfair Church of Christ in Oklahoma City. He was very quiet about his good deeds, but the speakers at his funeral told of his good works behind the scenes.

Charles William Jones made his transition into a new life on May 29, 2004.

CHARLES IN FULL ARMY UNIFORM

CHARLES AND MR. PIG

CHARLES JONES

VIOLET, REBECCA AND CHARLES

JAMES CUSTER JONES

James came into this lifetime on April 1. 1922. He was the fifth child born to the Jones Family. He weighted 12 pounds and had black hair and dark complexion. Daddy loved this look, because he said they were strong Jones genes. The fair headed, blue eyed children had Chase genes, which were inferior in Daddy's mind. James was dubbed J C early in life.

I was the only Jones kid born in the hospital. By then, Mother was out of names, so she named me after the nurse who assisted in my birth. Her name was Vera. I'm forever grateful her name was not Mehitabel. The day I was brought home from the hospital, J C came to the car and took me in his arms. I'm told he looked at me and said, "Little girl, none of the other brothers and sisters want you, but I do." Thus started a closeness between the two of us.

One day he and I were walking across the creek and a big snake crossed over in front of us. He looked at me and said, "Is that another one of your brothers?" Thus I became Little Snake and he was Big Snake.

J C excelled at sports, and especially baseball. He played on a Kiowa Indian team. He was dark enough, and unless someone knew him, his secret that he was not an Indian was safe. He bought me a baseball cap and took me along to most of his ballgames. Several times, I even got to be batgirl.

For many years the Jones Farm was tended by horses attached to plows. Peewee tells of a time when he took a drink of water out to the field. J C sat down to take a drink of it and rest for bit. He let the team of horses do a round of plowing alone. The old lead Bay horse just followed the furrow. Now, you can't teach a tractor to do that!

At the end of the day and at lunchtime, he had to take the horses down to the creek to drink. While he was taking off the rein on one of the horses, it stepped on his foot and just left it there. He said, "Get off my foot, you old son of a bitch." He turned around and there was Daddy. Daddy told him to bring a switch with him when he came back to the house. J C searched and searched and found a twig about four inches long. He gave it to Daddy to whip him with. It wasn't big enough to turn him over and whip his butt, so Daddy just pulled out his ear and whipped him there. The child abuse people had not set up shop at that time!

Somewhere around 1942, we got a tractor. Daddy took J C to drive it home. I think it was purchased in Hobart. Wherever it was, it was a long way to drive a tractor. I remember when it came over the hill. It was a J I Case and it was orange with its two front wheels together. We all stood in the front yard and admired it. The horses were happier than we were about it!

Violet said J C was the boss of Cache School growing up. He always got to choose the team and told the kids what they would play at noon and recess. She tells about the game that J C named "Dungeons and Dragons" that was played in the cellar. Violet said it was more like playing doctor!

J C had more girlfriends than you could shake a stick at. Once when we were at the Alden Alumni, Berniece was the MC. I think it was the year that we honored J C's graduating class. She asked the audience how many of the ladies there were in love with J C in high school. Almost every hand in the audience went up.

J C volunteered for the Air Force before he got drafted into the Army. He was a talented mechanic and spent most of his time at the air base in San Antonio. He was never sent overseas.

He met Reba Jean Lamirand at a ballgame. She later worked for our Dad in his grocery store in Carnegie. They dated for a few years, but he always had something going on the side. Reba got tired of it, so she started dating a guy from out of town. The shoe was on the other foot now and J C did not like it one bit! He cut Reba and her date off at the U-turn and got her out of the car and asked her to marry him. They went to Wichita Falls, Texas that night and tied the knot.

They moved to Weatherford, Oklahoma, where he worked as a mechanic at an automobile dealership. It was on route 66, so there was lots of business. Their first child, Donna Jean, was born there. Soon, they heard Boeing in Wichita, Kansas, was hiring. He got a job on the flight line and stayed there until he retired.

Three more children were born to Reba and J C, Roger Dale, Larry James and Jill Ann. There were anxious times when Larry developed polio. He was in and out of the hospital, but he finally beat it. One leg is smaller and weaker than the other, but it has never slowed him down. He has his own sound equipment business. Roger started a band called "Against the Grain" that has had a lot of success in the Wichita area. J C was so proud of the band and often traveled with them. He always had CD's to give away at the Jones Reunions. Jill owns a beauty shop, and Donna is a housewife.

We got the call that J C had a massive heart attack on December 23rd, 2004. Reba was in the kitchen and heard a noise and found him unconscious. She called Larry who called the paramedics. She was so upset, he had to call an ambulance for her too. James Custer did not recover. He died in the hospital on December 24, 2004.

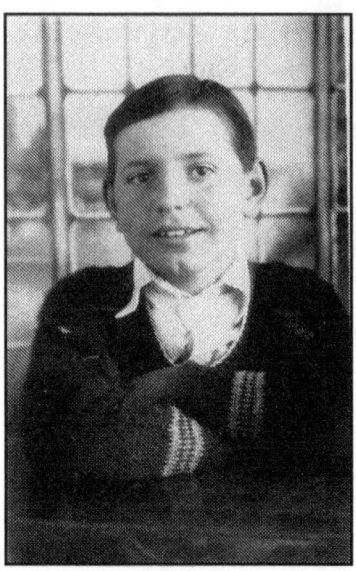

GRADE SCHOOL J.C.

JAMES C. JONES
U.S. AIR FORCE

NEWLY WEDS J.C. AND REBA

DONNA   ROGER   LARRY   JILL   J. C.   REBA

VIOLET HAZEL JONES MULLINS

Violet was in the only girl in between six boys, three older and three younger. She feels like she was spoiled being the only girl in the midst of all those boys.

After Violet's husband retired, they attended Elderhostel Classes to learn about many different topics. One that they attended was on writing and Violet wrote about herself and called it, "The Blooming of Violet." I thought it was pretty neat, so before I tell about her grown up life, here is the Readers Digest Version of her own story:

Cache School, a one-room grade school in Caddo County, Oklahoma, was the center of my social, educational and religious life. It was more than simply a school. It served as a place for Sunday School and Sunday Evening Gospel singing. My Father taught sight-reading singing for two weeks in the Fall, which all of us had to attend. Sometimes preachers would hold a revival there and we would have to go sing at it.

My first day of school was a happy one. Miss Dawes, a heavy set, loving teacher was there to greet us. She rang the big brass bell, calling us to line up. The first grade was in the line first. We were greeting by a big potbelly stove. In the winter, the stove would get cherry red, warming hearts, as well as the room. My desk was ready to greet me too. It was mine! It was ready for my books, crayons, paper and pencils.

At the top of the desk was an ink well and a place for my pencils. We all stood to salute the flag and sang, "America" and "Good Morning to You". There was a lot of energy in the room. It was still warm out, so Miss Dawes opened the double doors and we could hear the crows. It would soon be time to harvest the pecans.

You could smell the bologna and sausage sandwiches. The lunch and coat closets were close to my desk. Sandwiches were often exchanged. Poverty extended to a child's lunch box. Times were hard as we were in the Great Depression. A lot of the children's parents were sharecroppers.

All holidays were celebrated, but Christmas was joyous! There would be standing room only for the Christmas Program. We sang Christmas Carols. The tree smelled so fresh as it was cut from the neighboring mountains the day it was put up. We strung popcorn and cranberries for the decorations. Everyone got a red mesh bag filled with nuts, candy, an apple and orange. The peanut brittle was one inch thick and delicious.

Springtime was so welcome. The two big front doors were opened once more. We would hear the Meadowlark and Mocking Birds singing. We could see the dogwood and plum trees on the Steckman Farm blooming. Mr. Steckman was a small man with a large moustache. He was always so kind to me.

The last day of school was a community picnic. Mrs. Bowlin brought her burnt sugar cake and Mrs. Walters made an angel food cake. My mother always made the fresh lemonade. No one could make lemonade like she could. Of course, there was fried chicken, potato salad and baked beans.

Cache School was a conditionally or growing time of my life socially, educationally and for my soul. I did not start to school until I was seven, because I was too shy. It was the start of the blooming of

Violet! It was hard to leave Cache for Alden High School, but I adjusted and it was the last stage of the blooming of Violet.

When I got to Alden, I sang in the choir, played first base on the softball team and this is when I got my first pair of pants. I won the American Legion Award for the most outstanding student. I was voted, "Queen of the Fall", and was salutatorian of my graduating class.

And thus ends the telling of the blooming of Violet. For her graduation, Eileen sent her a new dress and ticket to come to California on the Greyhound Bus.

Violet was a little bit 'ornery with Berniece and I while we were growing up. One time she went to a "shiveree" (A party for newly weds where they sort of roast them, by trying to get them apart and do tricks on them). As part of the festivities, the groom gives out cigars. Violet got one and brought it home with her. The next day she took us out on the south porch and told us she was going to teach us how to smoke a cigar. We got to puffing and blowing out smoke and having a good old time, then the nausea hit us. We both threw up our guts while she stood on the porch and laughed at us.

Recently Berniece took me to see the stage play musical, "Little Women". At intermission, we recalled the time Violet read that book to us along with "Uncle Tom's Cabin" and a few other sad stories. The three of us slept in the same bed and she would read to us before we went to sleep. When it got to a sad part, Berniece and I would get under the covers and cry. She would tease us and ask us why we got under the covers. We loved having her read to us anyway and we eventually learned to cry above the covers!

Violet was the caretaker for Berniece and I when Mother went somewhere, so she thought up things to amuse us. One time she told us Mother had made ice cream and it was in the icebox. She got a spoon and said we could have a bite. This was during the war, so of course it was not electric. Sometimes we would buy blocks of ice to keep things cool. But being little farm girls that were not used to modern conveniences, we weren't smart enough to know that ice cream needed refrigeration, and a block of ice would not freeze anything. So, we dug in and spit it right out. It was a bowl of freshly churned butter!

Violet was a good student, but there was no hope of going to college, so she headed to California to get a job. On the bus to California, there were some soldiers who kept harassing her, wanting her address and phone number and to sit by her. She had dark hair and dark eyes and was very striking to look at. The first time the bus stopped for a rest stop, a sailor by the name of Bill Mullins, got hold of Violet's arm and steered her to a seat with him. He told the soldiers the sailor was in charge now and to leave her alone. (Bill had been on a ship in Pearl Harbor when the Japanese attacked, but fortunately he survived.) If you don't think we have a destiny in our lives, this may change your mind! He took care of her all the way to Los Angeles. She was impressed enough to give him her address and invited him to sister Yvonne's wedding that was coming up July 4th. He was so nice and kind to her. He showed her where to catch the bus to Torrance. She missed her stop in Torrance and did not know what to do. A girl riding on that bus asked her who she was going to visit and another miracle happened, as this girl worked with Eileen and Yvonne. There were no phones, so she took Violet home with her to spend the night and then took her to work with her in the morning. Eileen and Yvonne were worried sick, but did not know what to do, so they were very happy to see her.

She got a job at the factory where the sisters worked. She worked on a rivet machine kind of like "Rosie the Riveter"! She worked there for eight months before she returned home to Carnegie to work in Daddy's grocery store.

Bill showed up for Yvonne's wedding. He was stationed in San Diego, so he was close enough to visit from time to time. They hit it off and made plans to see each other again. After Violet went back home, Bill was stationed in Albuquerque, New Mexico and he came to Carnegie to see her and to ask her to marry him. I fell in love with Bill too. He was such a gentle spirit and he paid all kinds of attention to me. I called him Big Fox and I was Little Fox. I don't know how that came to be, but it lasted through my high school years. Sometimes when I send him a birthday card, I will address it to Bill Fox, from Little Fox.

Bill was in school at the University in Albuquerque, compliments of the U S Navy. He was commissioned as an Ensign when he graduated. They made plans to marry after his graduation in Albuquerque, so Violet took the bus and went to him. She stayed with the Congregational Minister and his family until the wedding. Next day after the wedding, they got a sleeper on the train to Seattle where Bill was newly stationed. She got a job at Woolworth's after they got settled. The first day at work, Bill showed up in his uniform and told her he got orders to ship out, so she had to quit before she got started. She took the train down to Torrance to stay with Eileen while Bill was at sea.

When Bill got back from his sea duty, he was stationed at Mare Island in Vallejo, California. While they were there, our brother, Claude, who was badly wounded in the Philippines was in the hospital at the Presidio, in San Francisco. His arm was badly damaged, along with shrapnel all over his body. After his surgeries and when he had regained some strength, the doctors let him have a leave to go see the parents in Oklahoma. Violet accompanied him on the bus. She said he was very weak and she had to hold onto him. Again, there were lots of soldiers on the bus and kept hitting on Violet. She told them she was married. One slipped his address to her and said, "If anything ever happens to your husband, here is my address."

In October, Bill was released from the Navy and enrolled in Texas A & M on the G I Bill and got his bachelors in Electrical Engineering. Violet worked in the cafeteria as cashier and hostess.

The University in Albuquerque invited him to teach there and he did for two years. Violet worked in a small café there. After that, he went to Stanford where he got his Masters. In June of 1951 he went to work at Hughes Aircraft in Culver City. He earned several patents for Hughes developing radar systems for aircraft. He retired after thirty-five years.

They got an apartment in Culver City and Violet finally became pregnant after trying for years. In preparation for having a family, they bought a house in Manhattan Beach. Chalon Glen was born in 1952, followed by Chris William in 1955. They got Carrie Gwen in 1957. Chalon is a computer architect, Chris is a High School English Teacher and Carrie is a Customer Service Agent for an airline.

After the children started to school, Violet started to El Camino College to work on her degree. She graduated with honors and went on to Long Beach State where she earned her Bachelors in History with a minor in psychology and Ethnic Studies in 1972. It took her a few years to complete, but she hung in there and finished bit by bit while managing a household of five.

She was area manager for the World Book Encyclopedia School Division for about ten years. She was and is very active in the Democratic Party. She was Assembly Chair for South Bay for four years. She was a delegate to New York City Democratic Convention when Clinton ran for President.

She has been a volunteer for Trinity Hospice for fifteen years working with the dying and their families. She has received many letters of appreciation from Trinity, as well as from the families she assisted. She was featured in the South Bay Daily Breeze as a Bright Light for her work with the hospice.

She was recognized by AARP as National Volunteer of the year. She was President of Manhattan Beach Sister City Program with Santa Rosalia, Mexico. She headed a book drive for students in Mexico.

She is a volunteer for the Community Concerts of South Bay area and she is neighborhood watch captain. I guess the old axiom, "If you want to get something done, find a busy woman" is true!

She has had to slow down somewhat the last year as her husband of sixty years was diagnosed with Alzheimer's Disease. He is doing well, but there are those moments! It is so sad to see such a brilliant and gentle man when he gets confused. The doctor told Violet that people with high intelligence sometimes progress slower. We hoping this is the case and he can maintain until a cure is found.

MISS VIOLET HAZEL JONES MULLINS

MISS VIOLET HAZEL JONES

HS GRADE VIOLET WITH ASSISTANT BUDDY HARDING

MR. AND MRS. W. H. MULLINS ON WEDDING DAY

VIOLET   CHALON   BILL   CHRIS   CARRIE

VIOLET AND BILL LIVING IN JAPAN

PRESIDENT VIOLET MULLINS MANHATTAN SISTER CITIES

DELEGATE VIOLET MULLINS NYC 1992

JOHN RALPH JONES

John was and is the comedian of the Jones Family. It's hard to have a serious conversation with him, because he will have you laughing somewhere in the midst of it.

As a child, John had heart palpitations, which would scare him and he would start running. Eileen said he would holler, "Naneen, come and catch me, I am going to faint." He grew out of the fits, but later did have some heart problems, which required open-heart surgery.

He doesn't have much memory of his early childhood. He remembers starting to school. He and Wad were always scuffling and getting in wrestling matches. He tells me of the time J C had organized a football game on the front yard. J C was always the boss and he and Wad got tired of it, so they had a huddle and decided to tackle J C and take him down. John told me that ended the game, but they felt they bested J C for once!

Before we got the tractor, John also did farming with the horses. He incurred Daddy's wrath while cultivating cotton and hit the manual lever too hard and took out a bunch of cotton. When we got the tractor, life became much easier. I can still see J C driving the thing down the hill into our driveway while we all stood outside and watched him coming.

John was the butcher of the family. Back in the days before all the government standards for meat, we butchered beef and hogs that we raised to sell in Daddy's store in Carnegie. It took a lot of courage to shoot the animal, then skin and prepare the meat. Surprisingly, we did not eat much red meat. When John butchered, Daddy let us keep just the liver. Mother knew how to fix it so it was edible. J C was the tender hearted one of the family, even though sometimes he was a bully. When John tied the animal to the tree to shoot it, J C ran in the house and covered his ears.

John had a best friend, Ham Bone Harding, who lived up on the hill from us. They were always going 'coon hunting down on the creek after dark. I could see their lanterns through the woods. I don't think they ever got a raccoon, but they got lots of squirrels and at least one skunk! On one of their hunting trips, our little dog that we named Poodle followed them out. (Daddy brought Poodle home to us in his coat pocket, so you can see he was small.) Anyway, Poodle got his collar caught on the fence and the boys didn't see him. We missed him for a couple of days, so the boys went out looking for him and found him hung on that fence. That was a very sad day for all of us. We had a funeral service and buried him in the corner of our vegetable garden.

John and Ham Bone went to West Texas to hire on for the wheat harvest. A lot of the farm boys did this, as it was about the only way to make a little money. While they were there, they got a case of Black Hawk beer and some cheap wine and hid it in our barn. One night, they were in the barn and Wad was with them and he drank a little too much. He went to the door of the barn and hollered, "Come on out here Lem, I want to whip your butt!" Fortunately for Wad, Daddy didn't hear him!

John has a slight impediment in his speech, which I think held him back from doing some things. No one had heard of speech therapy in our little community. He participated in sports in high school, but he was not a star. He told me one time he was practicing free throws in basketball. The star of the team yelled, "There's ole John Jones trying to hit a basket." Little remarks can scar a person for life and he said he didn't try much after that.

He has a great singing voice and has always led singing in church. He was the lead voice in the Jones Brothers Quartet and any time we are all home, we always sing and he is our leader.

One day, my best friend, Ellen Mulherin, and I were across the creek to bring in the cows for milking in the evening. In the middle of the field there was an enormous haystack. There came cries of "Help me", from this haystack. We climbed the fence and ran as fast as we could and started digging. John popped out of his hiding place. We could have killed him. He loved to pull pranks, but this one made us so mad, we ignored him for several days. I saw Ellen at the Alden High School Alumni in 2005. Our class was one of the two classes honored and it was so good to see her after many years. After we hugged and talked a bit, she reminded me of this incident. She said, "I'm going over to where John is standing and give him a piece of my mind for doing that!"

John got his notice from Uncle Sam in 1945. Fortunately, or unfortunately, the day before he was to report, while running after a cow, he tripped on a big rock and badly twisted his ankle. This caused his ankle to swell very large. When he went to Oklahoma City to be mustered into the United States Army, the Doctor asked him how he was. He said, "Fine, except for my ankle." The Doctor took a look at it, then went and got another Doctor to look at it. They decided he should go back home. He got his second call up in 1950 and this time, they took him in. He was stationed at Fort Benning, Georgia, then was sent to Germany for the remainder of his service tour. He returned to the farm in 1952.

After he returned, a wildcat oil speculator hired him to work on an oil rig and drill for oil. They drilled on several farms in the area, but never hit the big one. After this job slowed down, John went to Wichita, Kansas, where brother J C helped get him a job with Boeing Aircraft.

It was at Boeing that he met Ruth Phillips, a divorcee with three children, Raymond, Marie and Penny. She was really his first love and they got married and set up housekeeping in Wichita. They increased the family by three more sons, Michael, Steven and David. Times weren't always easy with 6 children. At one point, he was laid off from Boeing, and they returned to Carnegie and worked on a farm south of our farm where they were supplied with a house.

Work picked up at Boeing after several years, so they moved back to Wichita. When he was laid off again after a few years, he went to work for a plastics company and eventually retired from there.

Ruth became ill after all the children were out of the house, except for David, the baby of the family. David and John cared for her at home until she finally went to her rest.

The oldest son of the John and Ruth union, Michael passed away from cancer a few years ago. I was especially close to him as he lived with me for a few months when he came to California.

John remained a bachelor for fifteen years. He puttered around the house, planted big gardens, and was active in the church. It was here that he met Louise, who just happens to be from Carnegie also. They got married on Valentines Day 1994 and are still living happily ever after.

JOHN RALPH JONES

1ST GRADE

U.S. ARMY

HIGHSCHOOL GRADUATE

HAROLD AND JOHN MEET UP IN GERMANY

PENNY   MARIE   RAYMOND   RUTH   STEVEN   JOHN   MICHAEL

LOUISE AND JOHN

HAROLD EUGENE JONES

Harold was born February 28, 1928. He was ninth in the pecking order of the Jones clan. He and Peewee share the same birthday. As a rule, a new Jones was born every two years. Starting with Claude on December 25th, we will all have even birthdays one year and odd the next.

Harold was nicknamed Wad early in his life because of his body shape. He wasn't real fat, just very husky. He looked a lot like Hoss on the TV show, "The Ponderosa", and his personality was about the same, very friendly and loved by all. He loved to tell jokes and one of his favorites was: "Are you fast?" If you answered yes, he would say, "Catch that fart I just let and paint it blue."

When I was in first grade, he was in the eighth grade. Our little Grade School only went to eighth, so I don't much about his high school years as I was still at Cache. I know he was a great basketball player because I did get to go his games. He had to buy special shorts to wear, because they didn't have any uniforms that big. Once when J.C. was at one of his games, he overheard someone way that it was no wonder Alden had a good team, that big boy in the different shorts was recruited from Fort Sill. J.C. got a good laugh out of it and didn't bother to correct them.

Wad was drafted into the army during the Korean War. He took his basic training at Ft. Hood, Texas. The rest of his service was spent in Germany. He had his picture taken in a little Dutch suit with wooden shoes on a visit to Amsterdam. This was really a cute picture and we still have a copy.

On one of his travels in Europe, he got on the train and there sat Ronald Mead, who later became his best friend and who became part of our family when he married Berniece. That proves we should always be on our best behavior because we never know who we are going to run into!

He came home on Thanksgiving Day. We kept meeting the bus in Carnegie that morning, but he was a no show. He arrived in the afternoon with Charles and Rebecca. He had stopped in Oklahoma City and they brought him home.

When he was discharged from the Army, he returned to the farm. All he ever wanted to do was farm. He was not interested in going to college. He lived with the folks and took good care of them. He was very good to help with neighbors and they called on him a lot. Of course, the neighbors were good to help him also.

After I was married and took my new husband home for the first time, nothing was changed as far as our father was concerned. If you were a Jones Kid, you were expected to help out. This year, there was a big truck garden, mostly tomatoes. Peewee was also visiting at the same time. In the evening, when it got cool, Daddy got in the old pick-up and started honking. This meant, "Load up, you yahoos, it time to go to work!" So Wad, Peewee, Gary (My husband) and I jumped in the back of the truck and off we went across the creek to pick tomatoes. When Daddy went to the other side of the field to check the cucumbers, the tomatoes started flying. Gary never knew what hit him. The Jones boys had initiated the new addition to the family.

After Wad took over the farming, the cotton patch pretty much went away. All the slaves to chop and pick were married and away from home, so he planted mostly wheat and alfalfa. He sprayed the wheat with some kind of insecticide. A lot of the farmers around there got cancer and died. It was suspected that the insecticide he used had a lot to do with it. Also during this time, a cow that he was trying to vaccinate kicked him in the stomach. So between the two things, he became very ill.

He went to the doctor in Carnegie. They admitted him to the hospital. It was determined that he had appendicitis. He was told to go home and wait till it localized. He went home, but it never localized, so Daddy took him to the doctor in Anadarko. Again, he was hospitalized. By this time, he was starting to turn yellow. The diagnosis this time was jaundice. He stayed in the hospital for a week. They sent him home and told him not to smoke or drink and to rest and the jaundice would go away.

He just kept getting worse, so Daddy went to see the Jolly Boys who were the owners of the local newspaper, The Carnegie Herald. They were involved in Veterans Affairs, and they got Wad in the Veterans Hospital in Oklahoma City. They ran a lot of tests and discovered a large tumor attached to all his vital organs. They operated on him and just closed him back up, as there was nothing they could do.

I'll never forget the phone call Daddy made to us. He told us if we wanted to see our brother alive, we had better come soon. Four of the sisters that lived in Southern California got tickets to go right away. Two of the sisters, Eileen and Violet had never been on a plane before. We got in an awful storm coming into Oklahoma City and I thought for sure we were going to meet our maker before Wad did. He lasted exactly one month from the day he was admitted to the Carnegie Hospital. All of the Jones Children were there. We were tested for blood type and four of us were his blood type. They immediately transfused him with our blood and he did rally for a while.

We stayed with him around the clock. There were enough of us so no one got totally zoned out. The last day he kept asking for Mother. She was so sad and he was mostly in a coma at this time. It was hard for her to go in, but she did and I went in with her. He sat up in bed and started singing, "I'm Dreaming of A White Christmas", then he asked Mother to get in bed with him. She cried so loud and ran out the door and he fell back into a coma.

By this time, he was so ill that it was hard for any of us to go into his room. Violet's husband, Bill and Charles's wife, Rebecca took most of the duty to stay in the room. It was the two of them who were there when he died. He made his transition into a new life in March of 1962.

This was our first experience with death and it was a shocker for all of us, as well as the small community. We held his funeral at the First Baptist Church in Carnegie, as it was the biggest church around. The funeral procession to the cemetery was over a mile long.

Wad had kept his GI Insurance and Mother was his beneficiary. When he died, Mother and Dad were all alone out on the farm in an old house that should have been torn down years ago. It had no modern conveniences at all and both of our parents were getting up in years.

A man in Carnegie was building new homes for $8,000.00 and Mother had $10,000.00 from the insurance. She went to town and bought one. She told Daddy that she was moving to town and he could come if he wanted to. He did!

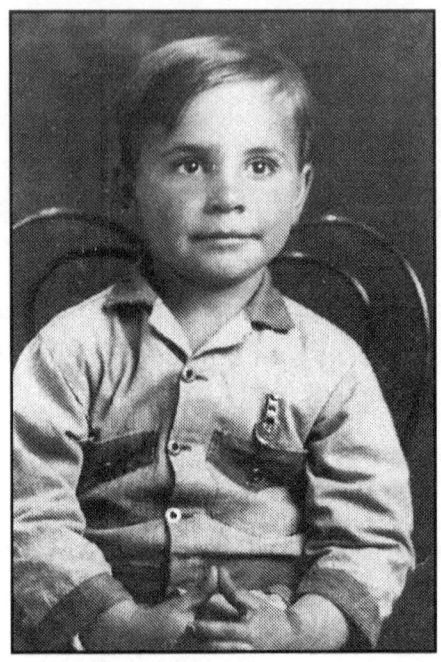

HAROLD EUGENE "WAD" JONES 1928-1961

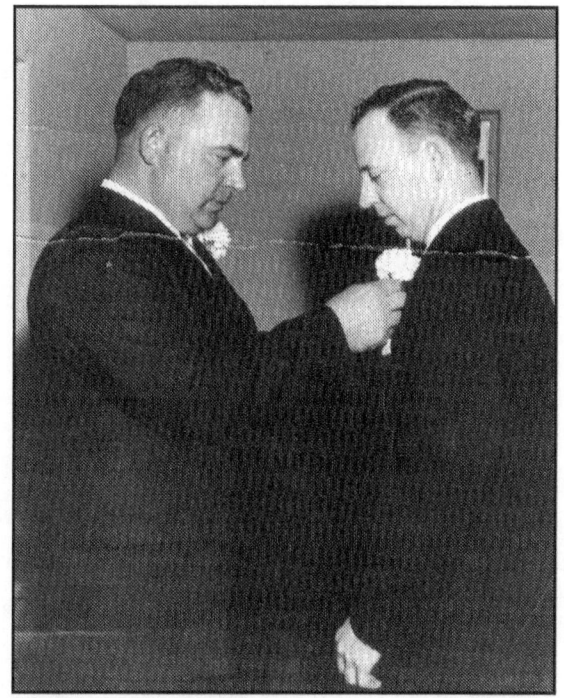

HAROLD AND DALE ON DALE'S WEDDING DAY

HAROLD

ROBERT DALE JONES

Robert was the last of the six Jones boys to be born. He was small from the beginning, so he was called Peewee. We knew him by Dale or Peewee. He was not called Robert or Bob until he was out in the work force.

Dale was fond of his Granddad Jones. When Granddad died, they laid him out in the bedroom at home, as was the custom in those days. Dale could not understand why he would not respond to him, so he slapped him on the face until someone saw him and stopped it.

The Jones children were born every two years. I suppose when Mother stopped breast-feeding, she got pregnant again. Seems they did not know about birth control! Before Berniece and I came along, he was the baby for four years. Mother thought she was done, but we came along and were called, "Change of life babies".

Dale wanted to go to school in the worst sort of way, so one day Daddy put a book in his hand and dropped him off at Cache School where his brothers and sisters were. He went up to the door and knocked. The teacher came to the door. She said, "Well, hello, who are you?' He replied, "I am Robert Dale Jones and I am in the fourth grade." Violet said she was so embarrassed when he came in. There was an empty seat on the front row. He strolled right over and sat down, opened his book and he was ready to go to work! He was such a cute little boy, no one could resist him.

When he was four, he got some brown paper and went out into the yard, rolled it up and lit it. It burned his tongue real bad! He liked to go on trips with Daddy and one time he sneaked in the car and hid. Daddy was half way to town when he saw Dale standing up in the back of the car. He had to call Mother when he got to town in case she missed him!

He also tells of the time when Claude was home visiting and he and Mother went with Claude to town. As they were going over a hill, one of the wheels fell off and rolled way off into a pasture. Fortunately they were going slow enough that it did not cause them to roll over.

When Dale was around seven, he was over across the creek with the older boys and our neighbors, Ham Bone Harding and Lloyd Bowlin. Dale climbed up in a tree. When he got up a ways up in the tree, he reached for another branch to swing over to. I think he was probably playing Tarzan. It was a dead branch and it gave way with him and he plummeted to the ground. He hit his head on an old axle lying on the ground. That is the last thing he remembered. Ham Bone and Lloyd picked him up and carried him home. He was totally out of it and they rushed him to the doctor. The doctor had a bed in his clinic and Dale did not wake up until the middle of the night when he heard a dog barking.

When he graduated from eighth grade at Cache School, he was the only one is the class. There was a time at Alden High School when there was only one high school graduate. In a small farming community like ours, all classes were small. I think my 1954 graduating class was one of the largest with nine.

The school district would not hire teachers that were married and the teacher he had was secretly married and the husband would come to the school after the kids went home. One day they hung around for some reason and caught them going at it.

The transition to High School was not hard for him. He was a good baseball and basketball player and there were sports to play all year long. Alden High School usually had good teams. There were so few of us in the school, that everyone who wanted to play sports had an opportunity. Bench time was less when there were fewer of you!

When Dale was a sophomore, Alden High offered a Drivers Education Class and the vehicle they used for training was a school bus. He said it was kind of hard to drive and the brakes were different and hard to get used to. But the whole class got their license. They didn't take the test in the bus!

Dale remembers the time he and Wad went to the Easter Pageant down in the Wichita Wildlife Reserve near Lawton, Oklahoma. They each took a girl friend and Bill and Violet were the chaperones. The pageant was famous in that area and it lasted all night. It was a great chance for "fool-around", especially if your parents allowed permission to go without them. Dale said he felt bad bringing his date home after the sun came up. The next year the parents of his girlfriend sent her away to school and the romance was ended.

During the war, we used to have groups of airplanes fly over our farm. Once a big bomber type plane flew over that we had not seen before and Dale jumped up on the cellar door to watch. The hinge gave way and he disappeared and the door flopped back up just like Houdini. It was like now you see him, now you don't. I thought he was killed and I ran and hid in the barn while they got him out. He was fine.

On weekends Daddy took Dale to work in the grocery store in Carnegie. He got no salary, but would help himself to change now and then. The Juniors and Seniors at Alden High sold candy during lunch time to help pay for the end of the year trip. We very seldom had money to buy one of those five-cent candy bars, but every once in a while, I would bug my brother for a nickel and if he had one, he gave it to me. What a brother!

Dale had a great singing voice, as did most of the Joneses. He performed solos at the school programs. He and his wife, Joyce, sang in the Church Choir and often did duets together. Joyce is a great piano player and singer. She sings with the Kansas City Symphony Chorus.

When Dale graduated high school, he worked on the farm and in the grocery store in town. When he was 22, he got his "Letter from Harry" inviting him to be part of the US Army. Dad got him deferred for awhile on hardship basis, because Harold and John were both in the service. John mustered out at Ft. Sill as Dale was entering in. We went down to visit and saw both of them.

Dale was sent to Louisiana for basic training, and then he was sent to Germany. Because he could type, he was assigned to be the company clerk. Later he became the supply clerk. On weekends, he and some fellow soldiers got on the train and did the tourist thing. There were lots of castles and local color to visit. He also got to go to Amsterdam, where he had his picture taken in full Dutch costume, as Wad did too.

When he got out of the service, he had $400 in savings. He got extra pay for unused furlough time, plus mustering out pay. He put it in the bank and let it grow. He bought a 1951 Ford for $375.00. Then he enrolled in Southwestern State College in Weatherford, Oklahoma. He got $110.00 a month on the GI Bill, and was able to finish college on that amount of money. His degree was in biology. One of his professors at Southwest had ties with the Institute of Technology in Kansas City at the KU Medical Center, and had recommended it to Dale. He applied before school was out and was accepted. He was trained here to be a Medical Technologist. He was paid a stipend of $85.00 a month, had free laundry and reduced dinner cards. It was here that a Pathologist began to call him Bob, and that is how he became Bob.

After a year, he took the registry and passed it. He stayed on at the Hospital and worked. Joyce McCalmon came to work here in January. One of the guys he worked with told him to go upstairs and see the new girl. So he did and was introduced to her. On Saturday, the supervisor asked Bob to work with Joyce, and he agreed to. After work, Joyce was at the bus stop when Bob drove by. He rolled down his window and said, "Hey little girl, would you like a ride?" She got right in according to Bob. They started dating. He was living in an old hotel that an old lady from Germany had converted to apartments. She furnished it from the Salvation Army. She told Bob, "When I was growing up in Europe, I was told the streets of America were paved with gold, and you know what, they are!"

Joyce and Bob were married in December of 1960 after dating for ten months. They became the parents of Melinda, Julie, and Kathy. Melinda has a son, Michael, who just graduated from High School and Triplet girls, Marion, Sarah, and Amy. Little Emily came along later. So they have five grandchildren. Melinda is a music teacher. Her husband, Tom, is an architect. Kathy and Julie do not have children.

Julie and her husband are tour guides at various National Parks and they also own a little store in Escalante, Utah. Kathy works for Verizon Cell Phones.

After leaving the hospital, Bob worked and retired from the Food and Drug Administration. Both he and Joyce work part time for the Johnson County Health Department as Medical Technologists. It keeps them young and allows for "candy money" to spend as they please.

ROBERT DALE "PEEWEE" BOB" JONES

US ARMY

JULIE   KATHY   MALINDA   BOB   JOYCE

BOB'S TRIPLET GRANDDAUGHTERS AMY, MARION AND SARAH

PFC ROBERT DALE VISITING HOLLAND WHILE STATIONED IN GERMANY

VERA, JOYCE AND BERNIECE SINGING AT ALDEN ALUMNI

JOYCE AND BOB

BESSIE BERNIECE JONES MEAD

This is the sibling I know most about, because she is next to me in the pecking order. She is a typical Pisces, a water sign with lots of emotions. Growing up, she was kind of a loner. I think she was really mad that she had to come back, as her wheel of karma was not completed. Mother said she cried nonstop for a week after she was born. This backs up my theory of her not wanting to return to Planet Earth!

When I was almost two, Berniece took me down to the branch where we had an old car buried in the dirt. It still had the steering wheel and we spent a lot of time in that old car make believe driving. We had a bunch of goats, because I was allergic to cow's milk. They always gathered around us when we went outside to play. I guess they bugged her too much, so she left me down there and went back to the house. She got in a bit of trouble when Mama finally got around to missing me!

Once Berniece was again down in the branch, this time by herself. She was about four at the time. She came running up to the house and told Mama the devil was down there. Mama asked her to show her where he was. She took Mother down there and showed her a bat. You didn't see bats much in the daytime, but I think this one must have been injured. Berniece was really relieved when Mother explained what a bat was and why we do not see them in the daytime.

Mother went to visit her mother in Little Rock, Arkansas. Her family did not really have much to do with our family. After all, we were a bit low class with eleven kids and no running water or inside bathroom. For some reason, she took Berniece with her and left me at home. When they got back, Berniece had a bunch of candy valentine hearts. She had them spread out on a chair. I wanted some so badly, but she would not give me any, so I went over and knocked them all off. She didn't get in trouble for not sharing, but I did for knocking them off, but it was worth it.

She always had the ability to make things last. If we were given a candy bar or a bottle of pop, I would gulp mine down, and then she would torment me by eating slowly. In all fairness, I think this was just her style and mine was more glutton, so I shouldn't blame her.

Grade school is kind of a blur. It went by so fast when it seemed so slow at the time. I was always outside being a tomboy and Berniece was more the domestic type. She helped cook and stayed inside mostly. She did go across the creek to visit a particular tree that she called Alta's House. I can still conger up a picture of her squatting down, digging in the dirt with a stick and talking to Alta. Now, I thought that was normal and just left her alone and rode away on my stick horse. When Eileen was home to visit and took a walk across the creek, she came upon Berniece talking to Alta. She just died laughing and thus the one episode was the end of Alta.

We used to sleep outside in the summer. All of us played the game of trying to count the stars, find the milkyway and seeing who could tell the biggest story. Before we would go to sleep, B and I would go down behind the hen house to pee. One night, all she had on was her unders. Her back was all white, and one of our old hound dogs came up and lifted his leg and peed on her back. She screamed and I couldn't quit laughing. The old dog came up so slowly and stood there for awhile before he lifted his leg. It was a shock when we realized what he was doing.

Now that I think about it we had a lot of magic in our life. We had two henhouses that had roosts in them. We used to get up on the highest one and do our business. We had an outdoor toilet, but no one much used it except Mother. To get to the outhouse, you had to go past the henhouses. We had this old Tom Turkey that was mean as sin. He would flog anyone who tried to walk by him. Once he was going to jump on Mother and she picked up a brick and knocked him cold. I thought Thanksgiving was coming early that year, but he survived.

There was a lot of rain and the cellar at Cache School got flooded, so the teacher took the older kids out of class to help bail the water out. She left Berniece and two little boys in the school, as they were too little to help. Berniece went to the outhouse. When she came back there were two little penises showing on each side of the door, a brown one and a white one. There was a bunch of horny little boys at that school and they were always doing something like that.

Berniece was always eight going on eighteen. She wanted to be grown in the worst way. We used to sit out on top of the cellar at night and count fireflies and daydream of what we would be and who we would marry. Then we would name our children. I would always look toward the west, because my heart was already in California.

One night, we were outside and Berniece was sitting on the cellar and Dale and I were tossing a ball in front of her. We looked over at her and she had her legs kind of spread out. We could see something sticking out of her pants that looked like hair. We put down the ball to get a closer look. She started running from us, so of course, we had to chase her down. We caught her and pulled her pants down. She had taken corn silk from the corn on the cob we had for dinner and pretended she had public hair. We have got a lot of good laughs over the years from that episode.

We used to go swimming in the nude, because we didn't have any bathing suits. If it were just the two of us, sometimes we would paint designer mud suits on our body. If we were swimming with Jimmy and Willie, who lived across the creek from us, we had a different plan. They would turn their back while we got in and we would look the other was while they got in. Same procedure when it was time to get out.

Once we were playing in the creek and Mother was with us sitting on the foot log. An old Indian came whistling down the path, so we ducked under except for our head. I think he knew we were nude, thus the whistling. He must have sat with Mother for an hour, while little by little we were turning into prunes!

Singing was a big part of the Jones Family's life. All of us could sing, but Berniece had the best voice. She sang at many school functions, as well as weddings, funerals and etc. She is still singing and accepts any requests to do so.

In high school, we had a very close relationship with our classmates. It was one for all and all for one. I think when there are only twenty-five students in the whole school, there is a bond that lasts forever. Of course, there are a few who never return to alumni gatherings, but most do.

Alfred Koehn had an old car and he used to pick up us and we would terrorize the neighborhood by honking the horn and hollering. Or maybe just go somewhere and park and talk. There was no smoking or drinking or drugs, but we had a heck of a good time.

When Berniece graduated high school, sister Violet and husband Bill came to get her. They took her back with them to California, where she would baby-sit and still be able to attend college. She went to El Camino Junior College in Lawndale, California. While attending there, she met a girl also from Oklahoma. Berniece asked where in Oklahoma she came from. She said, "Oh, its just a little town, you wouldn't know it." Berniece said to tell her anyway and she said Alfalfa. Alfalfa is north of Carnegie and Alden is south and we had great rivalry between our schools. Small world, isn't it?

While Berniece was attending college, she had an abscess in a front tooth and had to go around with it missing, until the crown came in. She rode to school with a neighbor who had an Arkansas tag on her car. The neighbor had an accident and the back door was missing. The two of them had a great time on the way to school. When someone drove next to them, Berniece gave them a big toothless smile. Can't you just hear those Californians talk about the beat up car and it Arkie occupants!

Berniece came home to visit at the end of her first year in California. I was really glad to see her, as I had no one to harass when she left. The first night she was home after we sat down to supper (Dinner was noon, Supper was night) the Railroad Hour came on the radio. I guess she forgot the rules that applied at our Father's Table. Anyway, she screamed out, "Woo-e-woo" like the railroad does. I thought to myself, "It's her first night home and Daddy is going to kill her!" He didn't say a word, just kept on eating. I guess that proves that time does change everything.

After two years in California and a lot of water under the bridge including illness and family problems, she returned to Oklahoma and came to school at the Oklahoma College for Women where I was attending. I moved from the freshman dorm to the sophomore dorm to room with her. I stayed in the same dorm for the next year, so I got ribbed a lot for being a sophomore for two years.

Berniece stayed here for a year, then she had persistent female type problems, so she went back to California where she had been treated before and wound up having to have an operation. She stayed there and went to work so she could save up to go back to college.

In the meantime, I graduated college and went to California to teach. She and I got an apartment on Signal Hill for $50.00 a month. After I got married, she went back to OCW in Chickasha, Oklahoma to complete her degree. She was popular there, even though she was a little older than the other students. She was crowned May Queen and had other accomplishments. When she finished, she came back to California and taught in the Westminster School District.

When Wad died, Berniece went back to Oklahoma to help the Folks. As they were getting older, she felt that it was where she needed to be. She signed a contract to teach at our old school, Alden. She had only five students. Those kids should have progressed greatly as the attention one could give with only five students was tremendous.

The night Wad died, his best friend, Ronald Mead, who was teaching in Dalhart, Texas, came to the hospital just as we got the news that Wad had died. Ronald was standing there and Berniece fell into his arms. She and Wad were the only two single Joneses and were very close, so she took his death very hard.

When Ronald came home for a weekend after B had moved back to Oklahoma, he called to ask her to go out for a coke. (His parents lived in Carnegie too) The rest is history. They married the next April after Wad died. They finished out the school year in their respective places and the next year, Berniece went to Dalhart to teach. After a being snowed in for three days, they decided to move to California. They came out for a visit in the summer and both were able to get teaching jobs for the next fall. So they moved and began their teaching career there. They both are retired from teaching.

They had two children, Jay and Jan. Jay had an unfortunate accident while working as a stunt man at Knotts Berry Farm. During a stunt where he did a back flip off the water tower, his head missed the mat. He has been in a coma since August 20, 1994. Berniece and Ron had just retired and sold their big home in Fountain Valley and bought a motor home and were going to be on the road for awhile. They had made one trip and came back on Thursday and Jay had his accident on Saturday. They lived in their motor home for two years following Jay from hospital to hospital. Jay's wife lasted about three months after the accident, then she filed for divorce, so the Meads have been his caregivers since then. A more dedicated couple you will not find. Ron goes up in the morning, Berniece goes up in the afternoon, and they both go back at night.

After living in a small space called a motor home, they found a four star senior Mobil Home Park in Tustin only five miles from the home where Jay now resides. I liked the place so much, I bought a home here also. It is very secure and no yard work to speak of. There is enough space to plant flowers and I have an orange tree in my back yard. You have almost as much room as a regular house, but much less upkeep and work. You can just lock the door and go and everybody watches out for you.

Jan lives in Wichita, Kansas with her husband, Bill and their two sons, Nathan and Nicholas. Bill was laid off the Boeing Company, so he and Jan are pursing college degrees. They got their AA this year with excellent grades and are now at Wichita State for their Bachelors.

In 1978, the Meads and I were attending Stanton Metaphysical Fellowship Church occasionally. There was a flyer about a lecture on Sathya Sai Baba, an avatar in Southern India. It said he did miracles such as Jesus did. I was outraged as I still had a closed mind. Even though we had left the Church of Christ, I was not open to explore other avenues. I was feeling that the church should be about love and forgiveness instead of fear and hate, and I was hoping there was more to the game of life. I was about to be divorced and I was in turmoil and searching. I didn't go to the meeting, but they did. Ronald is kind of an old Indian whose spirituality has nothing to do with church, and when he embraced Baba right away, it made me think about it.

Both Berniece and Ron immediately accepted Baba as an avatar and got active in the organization. They hosted many events in the large home they had. B became a regional director of the Sai Spiritual Education and is now the national director. She has traveled all over teaching teachers how to teach values and morality. She even went to Russia where she taught teachers in the Public School there. When the Principal was introduced to her, she started crying and told B that she had seen her in a dream and now it is real.

Berniece is called upon to speak in many different cities for the Baba Organization meetings and retreats. I have gone with her on several of the trips and she usually calls me up and we sing some hymns. In New York City, there was standing room only at the meeting where she spoke and we sang. She got a standing ovation at the end.

I have not become involved in the organization like they have, but I have been to the ashram, and I can tell you he is for real. Like anything else in life, it does not require belief, either it is or it isn't. Baba himself states he did not come to start a new religion, but to restore righteousness. He said every religion is a path and there is but one God. Be true to what you are, but respect the other paths. When you visit the ashram, you will see people from all countries and all religions. When we get the concept that he is trying to teach us, maybe then we can have world peace.

BESSIE BERNIECE JONES MEAD

AUNT BESSIE GRAVES AND NAMESAKE BESSIE BERNIECE

HIGH SCHOOL GRADUATE BERNIECE JONES

BERNIECE RIDING JACKRABBIT ON THE WAY TO CALIFORNIA

OKLAHOMA COLLEGE FOR WOMEN MAY QUEEN 1960 WITH PARENTS

FIRST YEAR TEACHER MISS BERNIECE JONES

BIRTHDAY PARTY FOR JAY MEAD

MEAD FAMILY
JAN   JAY   BERNIECE   RON

BERNIECE AND VERA 1937

BERNIECE AND VERA 1940

VERA AND BERNIECE 1952

VERA, VIOLET AND BERNIECE 1945

BERNIECE AND VERA CAUGHT IN THE SAME POSE

BERNIECE ON HER ADULT TRICYCLE LOOKING AT HER NAME ON
THE SADDLEBACK BIRTHDAY FLAG

VERA ANN JONES MOORE JONES

It was on September 19th, 1936 when I born. I was the first of the Jones eleven to be born in a hospital. Mother was 43 and not in the best of heath and was suffering from edema, so this was why Daddy took her to Elk City Community Hospital (An early type HMO). It was about 60 miles from our home. I came in screaming about 9:00 PM that evening. Mother's milk would not come down, so I was bottle-fed. (The other ten kids took all the good milk!) I was allergic to cow's milk and broke out in a terrible rash. Berniece has only one memory of me when they brought me home. It was of my red butt! She said it looked like a monkey's butt!

I was bathed and carried around a lot, but my rash would not go away and I was starving to death, as I could not digest the milk. So mother and I went back to the hospital. She for an appendectomy, and me to try to find some formula to save my life.

It was determined that I could not tolerate goat's milk, so before I could go back home, Daddy had to go buy some goats to feed me. There are lots of good stories with those goats. If the car was close to the house, they would jump up on the hood and get on the roof of the house. The house was so old and decrepit, it's a wonder they did not fall through the roof. I guess they got down the same way they got up!

A lot of things that happened as I was growing up have appeared in other parts of the book, so I'll just tell of my life after high school.

I always wanted to be a teacher, but to be a teacher, you had to go to college. I knew that was pretty much impossible, but a miracle was about to take place.

My Mother went to Arkansas to visit her mother. Berniece was already in California and since most of my time was spent in the field, I didn't know how to cook. Freda Johnson, who lived a couple of pastures over and was a life time friend, volunteered to come over and stay until Mom got back. Freda had just graduated from OCW and was going to be teaching in McFarland, California in the fall. The last day she was to be there at lunch, she said to my Father, "Mr. Jones, are you going to send Vera to college?". He looked over at me and said, "I guess so, if she wants to go." My world totally changed in that moment. This was on a Thursday and by the Monday of the following week, I started summer school at the Oklahoma College for Women, sixty miles from home in Chickasha, Oklahoma.

If I could can that moment and sell it, I would be a millionaire many times over. Can you imagine a farm girl, fairly smart, but without much hope, going to college? I thought I had died and gone straight to the top tier of heaven. I kept pinching myself to see if it were true.

This without a doubt, was the greatest summer of my life. It was my first time away from home, and I was totally in charge of what to do. I got a job in the cafeteria, but summer school was only in the morning, so we had playtime in the afternoon. I roomed with two friends that I knew from Carnegie High School, Rita Aston and Norma Lee Horton. We spent a lot of time in the student union and sipped a lot of root beer floats. I gained twenty-five pounds that summer, most of which are still hanging around!

Oh, the grand experience of college. Since it was a woman's college, most of our activities were rivalries between senior and sophomores and juniors and freshmen. We had play days to see who were the champions and a carnival to top it off and crown the winner. We had seven social clubs and rush week at the start of the new school year was a fun time. We had Spring Sing, Religious Week, and intramural sports. This was the first time I had played tennis. I was pretty good at it and played all through the years until my knees gave out. I still am close to a lot of my classmates at OCW and try to go back to reunions at least ever other year.

I worked in the cafeteria the first year and Mickey Morales and I did a lot of singing while washing dishes. I stole a chocolate cake with the help of Paul, the baker, for Berniece's birthday and we had a party in our room. She recently showed me a picture of that occasion and said, "Remember, this is when you stole that cake."

The rest of the time, I worked on the college switchboard. It was kind of spooky at night as it was in the hallway of the Administration Building and no one was there at night. Betty Ann Stout, my roommate, also worked there, so we kind of looked out for each other when it was time to sign off, as you had to go to the basement to close.

Betty Ann and I were a little bit on the ornery side. During Frosh-Soph week when we were the Sophs, we climbed the back fire escape and snuck into the Freshman Dorm. We were there to steal something that had to do with the rivalry, but I don't remember what it was. I think it was a flag of some kind. Anyway, Ma Netzel, the housemother was just around the corner. Some of the freshman girls saw us and knew she was tough, so they led us into the bathroom. We got on top of the toilet seat, shut the stall door, hunkered down and prayed she didn't see us. Our hearts were beating fast! She came into the bathroom, but fortunately for us, she did not open the door. That was a close call and I'm sure we would have been suspended.

I finished college in three years and three summers, as I needed to do it quickly and get to work. Daddy gave me as much support as he could, and of course I worked. My wonderful brother-in-law, Bill Mullins, loaned me the money for the rest. He is an advocate for education and my special angel.

I finished college in August of 1957. The college only had graduation once a year, so I am listed as a 1958 graduate. That is fine since it is the class I started with. I headed for California the next day. My sister Eileen Smith and her husband, Glen had sent their twelve-year-old son, Boyd, to the farm to visit. He flew out, but we took the train back compliments of the Smiths. That was one long train trip. The Porter came by and told me when Boyd went to sleep, to come back to his quarters. I was so terrified, my eyes were wide open all night. We pulled into Los Angeles early on August 1, 1957. Carrie Mullins had just been born that morning and the family was so happy, as she had two brothers, and they desperately wanted a girl.

The Smith's kept me until I got a job. They also financed me a car. It was a 1949 Chevy and I called her, "Bluebell Jones." I paid them $50.00 a month until it was paid for. Eileen took me down to Los Angeles Board of Education to be interviewed for a teaching job. A Principal, Helen Brandley, from Bloomfield School in Hawaiian Gardens was there and hired me on the spot to teach fourth grade.

Hawaiian Gardens is in the southwest corner of Los Angeles County. In 1957, it was a very poor socio-economic area, mainly Spanish. I didn't turn twenty-one until two weeks after school started. I was hardly equipped to handle what I was facing. I had forty-two students, one eighth were Spanish speaking only and about one eighth were not able to read. I could read, but I could not speak Spanish and I had quite an Okie accent. As the year progressed, I began to feel more comfortable. The next door teacher, Belva Allen, was a big help to me, as were the other teachers. We were a close knit group and that is how we existed. There was a café that specialized in pies and a couple of days a week after school was out, we walked down and indulged. It was acts such as this that helped me to keep my weight up!

The first Christmas I was there, I bought a Christmas tree for my classroom. I was going to Oklahoma for Christmas, so I asked my Class if anyone did not have a tree. Five hands went up, so we had to have a drawing. I put the tree in my car trunk and the winner in the front seat and we proceeded to his home. The streets were not paved and I hit all the chug holes, but we got there. When I took it inside, they had a dirt floor.

After my first year of teaching, my college roommate, Betty Ann Stout came to California to teach. She thought she was still in Oklahoma. When we walked down the street, she spoke to everyone and when no one spoke back, she got the concept! One place we went to see about renting a place, the owner of the house told us, " I don't like girls that date sailors (Long Beach had a Naval Base then) and I don't like girls that lose their keys." Betty Ann said, "Oh no ma'am, we don't date sailors and we don't even know any, and we never lose our keys." As we were walking to the car, we heard someone say, "Yahoo, girls, are these your keys?" Betty had laid them on her coffee table and walked out. We have laughed about this so many times.

We ended up renting a house on the Peninsula in Long Beach. After two months of living there, Berniece came down and asked if we would be willing to move to North Long Beach, which was half way between her job in El Segundo and our teaching jobs. We were right on the water and it was nice to take walks on the beach. However, the people on the Peninsula were not very friendly to outsiders (and the two

Okies were definitely outsiders!). Since we weren't real happy there, we agreed. The problem was we had signed a one-year lease. The owners told us if we could find someone to take it over, they would let us out of it. So, we advertised and three girls came down to look at it. They did not take it, but they stayed and visited. When they found out we were from Oklahoma, they went on about this guy, Gary Moore, that lived in their apartment. They did not give us their address when they left and they did not take over our lease.

We did find someone to take our lease over. We went to North Long Beach and found a place. We didn't have any furniture, but in those days furnished apartments were easy to find. When we were moving in, guess who was our next door neighbors! Yes, it was those girls. We did not even get unpacked before they wanted to take us over to meet Gary. I mentioned before that you can not escape your destiny and I was about to meet mine head on. He took to me immediately. When my parents came to visit at Christmas time, he came over to meet them. He said, "Glad to meet you, I am going to marry your daughter." I thought to myself, over my dead body! I married him the next August.

I taught in the Bloomfield School District for six years. At the end of my second year there, Gary and I got married. He was from Eastern Oklahoma. A true Okie born in Muskogee. I laugh when I think I moved from Oklahoma to get away from the men there and wound up marrying one.

We had a great marriage for the first few years. At least one weekend a month we took a trip somewhere. We had season tickets to the Los Angeles Civic Light Opera and enjoyed a good social life with my fellow teachers and the young married group at the Uptown Church of Christ in Long Beach. Gary was not a churchgoer, but he was baptized and was active in the church for a time.

After four years, we wanted to have children. We had done a lot of things by then and were ready to settle down. I couldn't get pregnant. I had surgery to correct some female problems and we also decided I should quit school and see if stress was the reason. If it didn't help, we would adopt. I got pregnant that summer and Melissa Ann was born in May of 1964.

We moved out of the apartment and bought a cute little two-bedroom home in East Long Beach. When I got pregnant with Marty, we bought a larger home in Lakewood. This was an estate home and it was a mess. We literally worked for the whole year fixing it up. After a year, we bought a four-bedroom home in Huntington Beach. We put in a swimming pool and it was a great place. Of course, the kids still wanted to go to the beach, instead of swimming in our pool!

By this time, my old roomie, Betty Ann, had also married. She and Curt bought a home in Westminster. It was the exact twin of our home, built by the same builder in those wonderful tract home days. We still tell each other we didn't like the house each other lived in!

Martin Lem came along the last day of December of 1966. Life was good and I was very happy. When the kids were older, I started substitute teaching. It was the perfect job as I left home the same time the kids did and got home about the same time.

I don't really know when things began to get not so good. Gary got a yen to move back to Oklahoma and kept bugging me to go. I love Oklahoma and like to go back to visit, but the opportunities are not there, and I was very happy in California. About this time, Missy was a rebellious teen and no matter what we did, it was not the right thing.

Gary left us once and moved back to Oklahoma by himself. It left me in a bad place, as I had to work, since he sent no support. The kids needed more supervision then I could give. I had to have knee surgery and was in the hospital for a few days. My sisters helped me with the kids. We had a crisis when I got home from the hospital. I had to send Melissa to a teen-problem home, as I could not cope being on crutches and trying to keep up with her. That night Gary called and said he was in Albuquerque on his way back.

I let him come back as I really needed help, but it was never the same. Then Melissa had another crisis, so I finally agreed to sell the house and move to Oklahoma. I told him I would go if he moved to Tulsa where some culture was available. The escrow on our home in Huntington Beach was a Cal Vet and it took 90 days. So Gary and Melissa left for Oklahoma right after Christmas, and Marty and I stayed. The day the escrow closed, Marty and I stood in the house crying. He said, "Mom, I do not want to go". I told him I didn't either, so we went out and got an apartment.

During those five months until Marty's school was out, Gary bought a house outside of Okmulgee, a very old town south of Tulsa. It was nice and on an acreage. He bought it without consulting me. I didn't have any say and didn't know about it until it was over and done. I was born and raised on a farm and I wasn't anxious to be out in the country again.

That summer I was going to give Okmulgee a try, but my Mother had a stroke and was near death. I sent Marty to Gary and Melissa came and spent some time with me. Mother didn't die, but was near death and in a rest home and I was attached to her and did not want to leave.

In September, Melissa went back to Gary and enrolled in school there. Mother died a month later in October of 1980. We took her back to Oklahoma to bury her in the family plot. That should have been my time to move, but as luck or fate would have it, I had an abscess tooth and had had the root canal, but the crown had not been made, so I went to the funeral and stayed a week in Okmulgee. When I returned home to have the crown put on, I felt like kneeling down and kissing the ground. I was so glad to be back in California. I knew this was not a good sign.

About this time, Violet and Bill were sent to Japan for a year. They called and asked me if I would consider house sitting while they were gone. I rationalized that one more year wouldn't hurt and I had a good job in Redondo Beach, so I stayed and moved to Manhattan Beach. (I had been living in Fountain Valley with Berniece and Ron.)

Gary and the kids came for Christmas and spent two weeks. I flew there for spring break. During this time, Gary agreed to sell and buy a place in Tulsa. While I was there, he went for a job interview in Tulsa. When he came home, he told me he flunked his physical because of discs in his back. He broke down and told me he didn't like it there and asked if he could come back to California. I agreed.

So after school was out they moved in with me at the Mullin's house. It is a very large home, so there was plenty of room. We enrolled the kids in Mira Costa High. It didn't fit well with Melissa, so they sent her down the hill to a continuation school. This was a turning point in all our lives, because she blossomed there where she could do it at her own pace. She took a course at ROP and was hired on at Little Company of Mary in Torrance to be a cardiology tech. She worked part time while still in high school. This gave her enough money to move out. After a few months, she signed herself up for a nine-month medical assisting course. I was proud of her, as she did it on her own and arranged her own financing. She did move back in with me while she was in school.

Things were sort of okay for awhile. Marty was on the football team and was doing well in school. When Marty graduated from high school, Gary got the Oklahoma bug again. I guess he figured the kids were old enough to take care of themselves, so he wanted to move back to Oklahoma. Marty decided to go with him. Melissa was already out on her own. This time I helped him pack and his move lasted. We mutually divorced and I took my maiden name back. He married once after we divorced, but that didn't last very long. I remained single.

I started attending meditation classes at the Metaphysical Church in Stanton to help me cope with the divorce. I, like everyone else who gets married, thought it would be for life, and some of my family gave me a hard time. No one in our family except for Claude ever got a divorce. Even if the marriage was bad, they stuck it out.

The church was starting a ministerial program, which lasted for three years. There was class every Wednesday night and you had to take part in a church service on Friday or Sunday night. I was talked into starting it and I had no intention of finishing, but it got interesting and I kept going. Three years later I was ordained. We had to give sermons and lead worship and do service while in classes. Since I could carry a tune, I led the singing and sang at special events at the church. I have no interest in having a church, but I have done a lot of weddings and a few funerals.

I could not find a full time job teaching, so I went to work in the business world. I have had great interesting jobs. I started with a British Sun Roof Company as Director of Transportation. This was before auto manufactories started putting sunroofs in cars. I would co-ordinate my drivers to go pick up the cars to install the sunroofs. When it was an expensive car, like a Rolls Royce, the owner requested I do the actual driving. And yes, Rolls Royce's do ride like you're floating on air. When Detroit got around to installing sunroofs at the factory, our company sold out.

The next thing was a dating service and I was Director of Processing.

We were a large company that covered most of the State of California and Phoenix, Arizona also. We gave our clients a battery of physiological tests and hand matched on seven attributes. I had a regional processor for each region under me, so I was kept very busy. The owner of the company was a very generous man. After our monthly processing, we would have a picnic or order special food in. He even hired a bus and took us all to Las Vegas one weekend. He let me take the company van and all my girls to the mountains for a retreat.

The company was actually started up in Detroit, Michigan. When the Director of Processing there took a maternity leave, I was sent to Detroit for four months. There were very big in that area and we had a lot of clients. The Person who was office manager there would not let the girls wear pants. I went there in October and the drive was absolutely beautiful with all of Mother Nature's fall colors. It got real cold in January, so I got brave and tested the "no pants policy". I wore a dressy pants suit to work. It didn't take long for the boss to call me into her office. She said, "We don't wear pants here." She had visited the office in California many times and knew we wore pants there. I responded that since it was a very cold climate it looked to me like dress slacks would be appropriate. She disagreed, so I told her I would go home and change and call the Department of Labor while I was at home.

Of course I did not call, but the next day she called a meeting and changed the policy that as long as the slacks were dressy with no jeans or casual pants, it would be allowed. I became a hero to those girls and stayed in touch for some years after.

A few months after I got home from Detroit, I was sent to Atlanta, Georgia to start up a new office. The couple who were in charge there were not very honest business people. They would come in the office at night and go over my work to learn how to do the matching. Then they made some matches of their own. The only problem was the clients already had the matches they made for them. I got to take the phone calls to try to save them as clients, and it was not very pleasant. Needless to say, it was not a match made in heaven and I threw in the towel and headed back to California.

By this time the computer had come along and some of the business practices of the eager salesmen got the company in trouble and they had to file for bankruptcy.

After the dating service, I got a job with a major airlines frequent flyer program as supervisor of customer service. I had great people to lead and great managers. There were a lot of funny incidents on the job. Once a member called up who had not got credit for his Hertz rent a car. He was very agitated and gave my agent a hard time. Finally, he was passed to me as an escalated call. I got it straightened out. I thought I had put him on hold, but the agent who had passed me the call was listening in to see how I handled it, so I could not put the customer on hold. I did not know that he was still on the line. I called out to Patrick, my agent, to put 500 miles in his account. But unfortunately, I said, "Patrick, do you still have that turkey's account up? Patrick said yes and put the mileage on the account. When I went back to tell the customer, he said, "Did you just call me a turkey?" I could not lie and say I did not, I just profusely apologized and said it was nothing personal, just for the benefit of the agent I took the call from. He accepted my apology. I was afraid he would write a letter of complaint, but my department also received the mail!

We were party animals similar to the dating service and I still keep in touch with a lot of them. This lasted eight years, then the union tried to come in. We finally defeated the effort, but management was afraid they would try again, so they laid us all off and moved to Arizona. I could have gone if I had been willing to take a seventeen-percent pay cut. Arizona is hot and I am menopausal, so I did not go.

The next two years were extremely hard. I could not find a job. By now I am in my fifties and don't let anyone ever tell you age makes no difference. One agency actually told me they were looking for someone younger. I could have made a case out of it, but I knew it was the truth, and the lady who told me that was my age.

I went through all the unemployment I qualified for. They even sent me to school to learn how to be a secretary. Then I had to use my 401K. I was on my last $100 when I got a job with a utility company. I will be forever grateful to them. It is one of the few companies that truly follows the no discrimination policy. I stayed there until I was forced to retire. New management came in and stirred everything up. I was in the Resource Pool and we answered correspondence and handled anything that needed special handling. My expertise was with the agencies and I was called "The Agency Queen!" When someone such as Catholic Charities, Salvation Army, Private City and State Agencies called in to made a pledge on a customer's account, I took the call. Then the agency would forward the money to me and I would make sure it was correct and forward it on to accounts payable for credit.

After being there for ten years and building a good relationship with the agencies, Management declared we should all go on the phones and let new people have a chance. I had one of the agents call me at home after I left to complain that everyone familiar was taken away, and the new ones were curt and sharp with them. I did not want to go back on phones and listen to people's complaints all day. When customers do not pay their bill and get their lights disconnected, it becomes our fault and the names they call us are not pretty!

After I retired, I was at loose ends. I had worked since I was five years old and what do I do now. Berniece and I joined a gym and were really getting fit and cute, when they sold out without warning and we lost the money we had invested with them. I read a lot. I wanted to travel, but didn't want to go alone. Most tours are based on double occupancy and I could not find a traveling companion. In short, I was depressed!

A chance encounter happened at a breakfast here in our mobilpark. I sat next to Will, who is assistant manager at our local mortuary. I told him I wanted to come down and answer phones for him. He called me two hours later to come down and talk to the manager. I was hired on the spot. I have progressed from answering phones, to traveling to doctor's offices to get signatures on Death Certificates. I also get to go the Health Department to file and get permits. Occasionally I transport a person on their final ride to the crematory. I sing hymns to them and talk to them. I hope they have some awareness and know that I care about them and the journey they are going on. It makes one wonder when it will be my turn to take that ride. I just work a few hours a week and since I am near by, they do call me in to help if it's busy. I have a lot of variety and it has really changed my outlook on death, as well as gives me money to spend as I please.

I started this book about ten years ago and could not find the energy to work on it until recently. There are so many funny things that happened growing up on the Jones Farm. I guess in reality it is an autobiography, but since I am not rich or famous, I just wanted people to have a good laugh, so I have finally finished it.

The other reason I wanted to do this was for my three grandsons, Miles, Preston, and Josh. I wanted them to know some history from the Jones side of the family. Miles and Preston are military children and move around a lot. Fortunately they were in California for several of my son's assignments, so I did get to be around them some. He is a Navy career person. His specialty was weather forecasting until 911 came along, now is in the Master of Arms, which is military police.

Josh is Melissa's son and they have lived with me for most of his life, so I do get to see them often. They live in Long Beach now, which is about twenty miles from me. Melissa teaches at St Francis Career College in Lynwood. They train people for careers in the medical field.

She teaches medical terminology, phlebotomy, and medical assisting, both front and back office. I am blown away by her knowledge. We could hardly get her to go to school and look at her now. It just proves that where there is life there is hope!

And so, the journey continues. As with any life there are ups and downs and all you can do is hope there are more ups. All the Jones kids are getting old. We lost J C and Charles both in 2004 and now there are six of us left. We try to get together as often as we can and the love we found hard to express in our formative years is now out in the open!

VERA ANN JONES MOORE JONES

FARMER GIRL VERA

GARY   MELISSA   VERA   MARTIN 1970

VERA   MELISSA   MARTIN   GARY 2002

TWO INDIAN MAIDENS, VERA AND MELISSA
AND ONE LITTLE COWBOY, MARTY

MELISSA AND VERA ATTEND A NAVY GRADUATION FOR MARTY

VERA BEING ORDAINED AS A METAPHYSICAL MINISTER

GRANDSONS PRESTON MILES JOSHUA

VERA IN HER BONNET

THREE GREAT REASONS FOR WRITING THIS BOOK - MY GRANDSONS

MILES HANOVER MOORE

PRESTON THOMAS MOORE

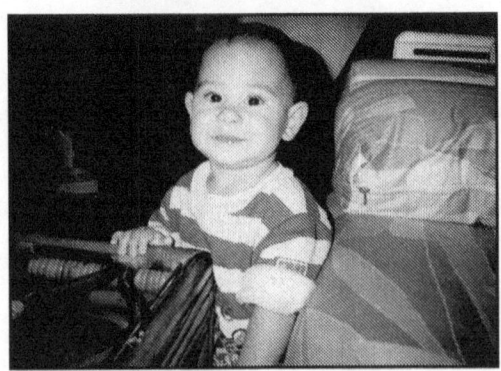

JOSHUA JAY MOORE

THE MELISSA MOORE FAMILY JOSHUA JAY AND MELISSA

THE MARTIN LEM MOORE FAMILY JENNIFER MARTY MILES PRESTON

VERA AND MELISSA

LEMUEL RASPBERRY "COON DOG JONES" IN CENTER WITH TWO HUNTING
FRIENDS AND 5 OF HIS 19 COON DOGS J. C. IS STANDING ON THE SIDE

EILEEN VIOLET CHARLES J.C. CLAUDE YVONNE JOHN
HAROLD DALE L.R. LOTTIE VERA BERNIECE

VERA, MOTHER AND BERNIECE ALL DRESSED UP FOR EASTER

DALE, VERA AND COONDOG ROWDY

DALE AND VERA IN MUD BATHING SUITS

155

CLAUDE   JOHN   CHARLES   J.C. HOLDING HAROLD

CLAUDE   CHARLES   HAROLD   JOHN   DALE IN FRONT

JOHN   VIOLET   CHARLES   J.C.

JONES FAMILY SINGING AT ALDEN HIGH REUNION - NOVEMBER 2001

BERNIECE J.C. EILEEN CHARLES VIOLET JOHN VERA DALE

JONES COUSINS AT J.C.'S MEMORIAL SERVICE - DECEMBER 2004